FOLD IT — FLY IT

A new dimension in paper planes

Dr Edmond Hui

Patrick Stephens

First published in 1988

British Library Cataloguing in Publication Data

Hui, Edmond
Fold it — fly it.
1. Paper airplanes
I. Title
745.592   TT174.5.P3

ISBN 1-85260-063-2

*Patrick Stephens Limited is part of the Thorsons Publishing Group,
Wellingborough, Northamptonshire, NN8 2RQ, England*

Printed in Great Britain by Woolnough Bookbinding Limited,
Irthlingborough, Northamptonshire

3   5   7   9   10   8   6   4   2

CONTENTS

INTRODUCTION

Commercial aircraft are designed to fly safely and efficiently, because human lives are at risk and because both aircraft and aviation fuel are enormously expensive. On the other hand paper aeroplanes, being totally harmless and ludicrously cheap, are rarely designed with any regard for their flying abilities. This has always seemed a shame to me, since regardless of size or expense all aeroplanes fly in the same air, and a paper aeroplane's performance can be improved with careful design every bit as much as the latest jet fighter. When built with a little thought, they can be made to circle and loop, providing hours of fun for children of all ages (even those drawing pensions!). There is probably no better way to relieve a moment's boredom in the classroom (or office) when the teacher (or boss) isn't looking!

Whether you have never made a paper plane or are looking for new ideas to improve your designs, you should find this book useful. Each step is fully illustrated so that readers of all ages can fly and enjoy all the paper plane designs without needing to understand any of the theory involved. I hope, however, that your curiosity will be aroused enough for you to tackle some of the simple aerodynamics that accompany the designs, and find out more about why paper aeroplanes fly.

This book aims to take you step by step from basic designs that are easy to make and fly, looking at ways of measuring how well they fly, through to the paperang, a paper aeroplane which performs well both in straight and aerobatic flight. Instructions are given on aerobatics, competitions and how to modify designs to fly faster, slower, or further. Aerodynamic ideas such as airfoil, washout, aspect ratio, lift and drag are introduced, with the help of simple do-it-yourself experiments to help you to understand the flight of the various designs and to invent new designs.

Paper aeroplanes have given me many happy hours of flying and I hope this book can help you do the same whether you have a degree in aeronautical engineering or have never tried to make anything fly before. Finally, thanks are due to Geoffrey, who started me folding and flying; and to Sandy, my wife and in-house editor.

Edmond Hui
Isle of Wight

1
PAPER AND PAPER FOLDING

Making paper aeroplanes requires no special skill, but the more care you take to build them accurately, the better they will fly. Please read these general instructions first, before you try building the designs in the rest of the book.

Paper

All the designs in this book are made from A4 (297 × 210 mm) paper. The paper should be as light as possible, but should also take creases well. The lined paper sold for writing works fine, but the rather heavier plain paper for drawing and typing is less satisfactory. Do not worry about holes if you use file paper, because they are usually hidden away in the folds, and even when they show they often have no noticeable effect on flying performance.

Folding

Diagrams will be used to show you where on the paper to make folds and which sides of the paper to bring together.

Figure 1   The scissor symbol will label a line where a cut is required.
A dotted line will indicate that a 'valley' fold is to be made. Imagine that the dotted line is actually drawn on the paper; it should end up on the *inside* of the fold.
A dashed line will be used when a 'peak' fold is required. Again, imagine that the line is drawn on the paper and it should end up on the *outside* of the fold.

Figure 2   The original top surface of the paper will be shown white and the reverse side shaded throughout the diagrams. When you are folding the paper, take care to line up the edges first, and hold them in place with one hand while you flatten the fold carefully from the centre outwards with your other hand. Do not flatten the fold from one end to the other since this introduces errors.

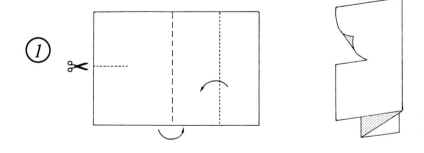

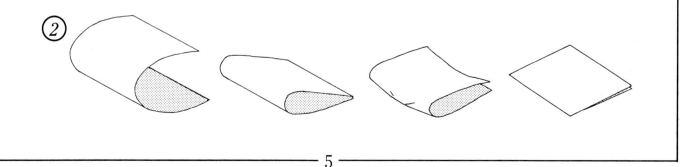

2

THE DART

When people think of paper aeroplanes, the design that most often comes to mind is the paper dart — something with roughly triangular wings coming to a pointed nose, with a V-shaped triangular keel. Despite their crude aerodynamics, darts have their good points: they are very easy to make and fly, and although there are planes that can fly further, or faster, or both, they are a useful and fun introduction to this safest and cheapest form of aviation. This is the basic paper dart that most people have come across.

You will need
1 A4 sheet of paper

Here's how to build it

Step 1   Fold the paper in half lengthways. This fold will be the keel of the dart.

Step 2   Bring one of the short edges down to meet the centre crease, and flatten along the dotted line.

Step 3   Bring the edge of the fold created in step 2 down to meet the centre crease, and flatten along the dotted line.

Step 4   Repeat the process one more time, flattening along the dotted line.

Step 5   Repeat steps 2 to 4 for the short edge on the other side to form the shape in the diagram.

Step 6   Open out the two wings to form the final dart shape.

Even with this simple design, you can see a little of what makes all paper planes fly — wings that spread horizontally to produce lift to counter the pull of gravity, and folds that stiffen the paper and hold it in shape. To fly the dart, just point it slightly downwards and launch gently — most people who make this design make the mistake of launching it very hard like a javelin, which only results in fast, uncontrolled crashes. Like most paper aeroplanes, it needs to be launched at its natural gliding speed to perform at its best.

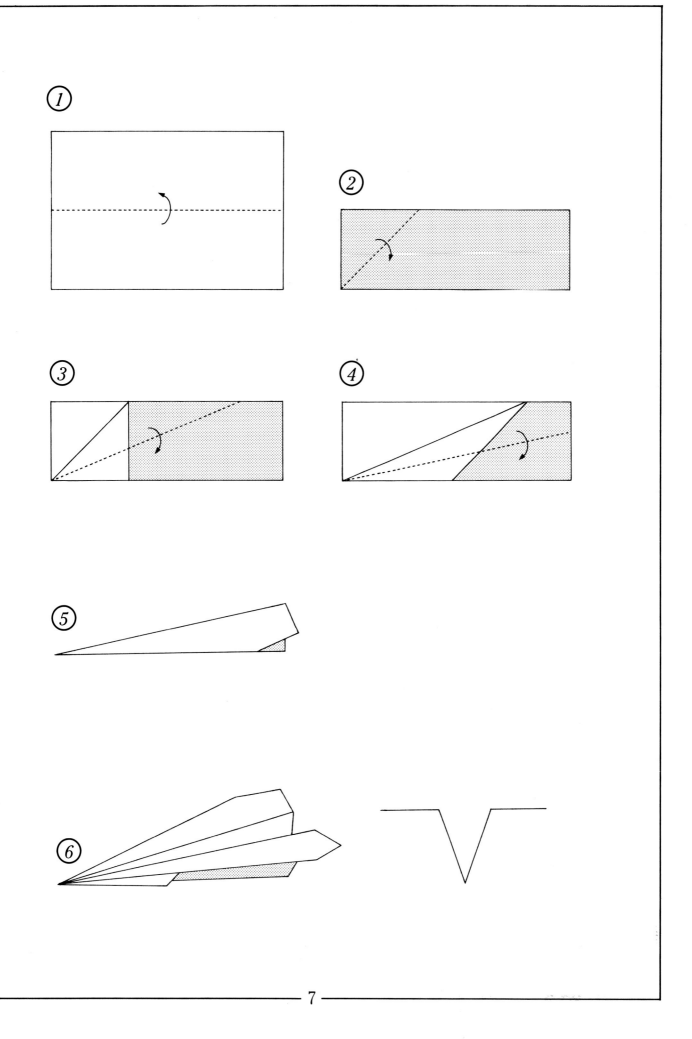

3
THE SHORT DART

You may have noticed that the folds of the long dart tend to separate in flight. The short dart uses a little tab to hold the folds together, creating a stiffer dart.

You will need:
1 A4 sheet of paper

Here's how to build it

Step 1   Fold the paper in half lengthways.

Step 2   Fold down the two corners at one end, one on either side of the centre fold.

Step 3   Open out the centre fold, and fold the pointed end down along the dotted line. The gap between the edges of the flaps and the new fold should be about 12 mm.

Step 4   Fold the corners down, and hold them down with the centre tab, which should be about 12 mm long.

Step 5   Refold the centre crease so that the centre tab is on the outside.

The wings of the short dart are made in two ways:

Type A
Step 6A   Fold the wings parallel to the centre crease, and form vertical tip plates with further parallel folds.

Step 7A.   Open out as shown.

Step 8A   The wings should be horizontal and the tip plates vertical.

Type B
Step 6B   Make the wings by folding the front edges down to meet the centre crease.

Step 7B   Open out as shown.

Step 8B   The wings should be horizontal, the keel opened out to form a right angle down the centre line.

Step 9   When you launch the completed dart, make sure that the top and bottom surfaces are held together, by grasping it by the little triangular flap.

When you fly these two darts, look at their path through the air. How do they fly? How do they differ?

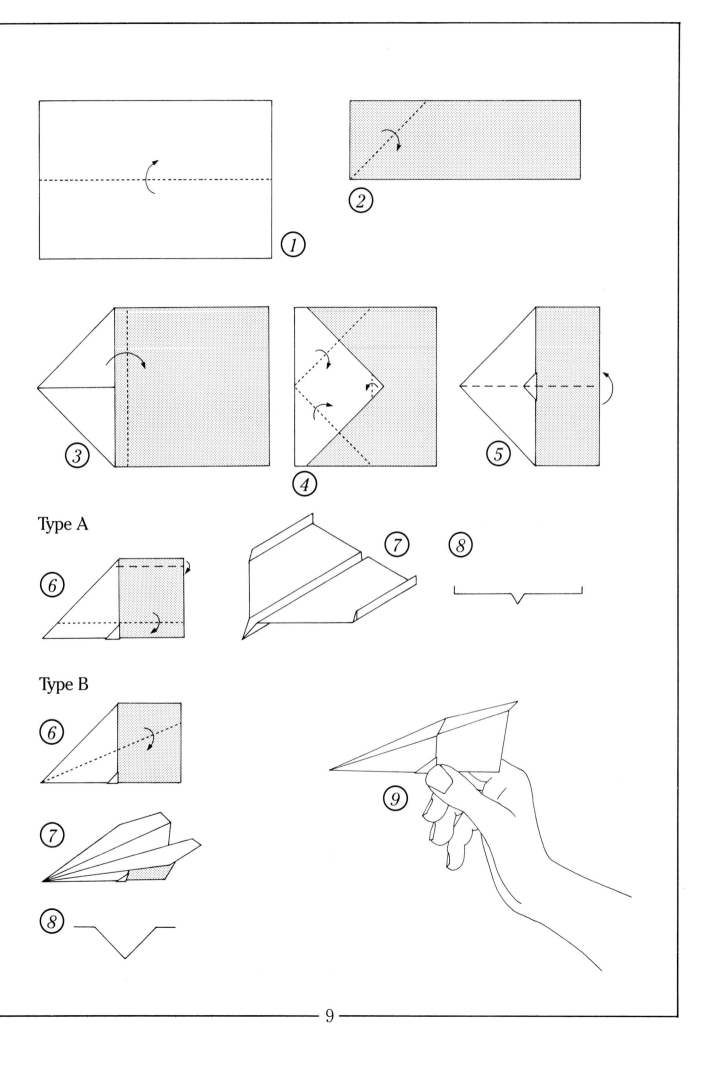

Type A

Type B

4

FLYING THE DARTS

Paper aeroplanes do not often perform perfectly on their first flight. The adjustments described below should help you to achieve a steady, straight glide.

Try launching one of the designs you have just made, and watch its flight. If the plane does not fly straight, try to spot and carefully straighten any inaccuracy, such as a bend in one of the wings, and test fly again. If it still does not fly straight, does it turn left or right, does it dive or follow a roller-coaster flight path, climbing slightly while slowing down, then diving and speeding up (Figure 1)?

Turning

If the plane turns left on the test flight, you will have to bend one of the vertical surfaces of the plane to the right. This pushes the tail of the plane to the left in flight, correcting the turn. (These bends work in the same way as the control surfaces of full-sized aircraft.) Figures 2 and 3 show how this is achieved on different designs.

The tendency of the plane to turn depends in part on how much the wings are swept up, ie the dihedral (Figure 4). The more dihedral there is, the more likely it is that the plane will keep flying in a straight line. If the plane is difficult to trim, tending to turn one way then the other on successive flights, try increasing the dihedral.

Stall and dive

Once the plane flies without turning, we can deal with its tendency to stall and dive. To cure a dive, try one of the adjustments shown in Figure 5 as appropriate. These adjustments tend to push the tail downwards, correcting the dive. A plane which roller-coasters is stalling. This is caused by the centre of gravity of the glider being located too near its tail. Add weight in the form of a piece of Blu-Tack to its nose.

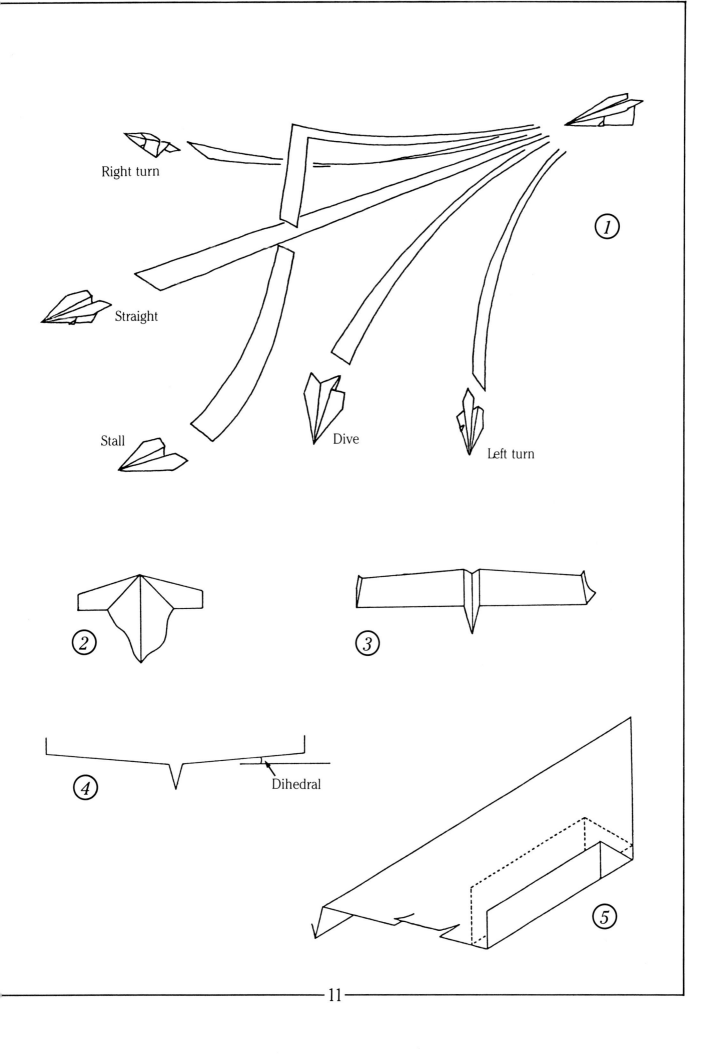

Right turn

Straight

Stall

Dive

Left turn

Dihedral

5

PERFORMANCE MEASUREMENT I

You can only improve the design of paper planes if you can measure how well they fly. Two measurements that will help you to do this are glide ratio and sink rate.

Glide ratio

The easiest way to measure performance is to see how far a plane flies. Obviously, the higher the launch the further the flight, so we would have to launch from a measured height. Glide ratio is given by the distance flown divided by the launch height so it takes into account both height and distance.

Figure 1 If you launched a glider from a height of 2 m and it touched down 8 m away from you, the glide ratio would be 8 divided by 2, that is 4. The more efficient the glider, the bigger the glide ratio. The path taken by the glider is called its glide path and the better the glider, the shallower, ie the more horizontal, its glide path will be.

Figure 2 Try measuring the glide ratio of one of the darts when it is launched from shoulder height and again when you launch it from a chair or step-ladder (be careful!). You ought to find that the answer will be about the same both times.

Sink rate

The time a paper plane takes to drop a certain distance is also a good measure of its efficiency. The lower the sink rate, the longer a glider will stay in the air. Sink rate is calculated by timing the glider from launch to the moment of touchdown, and dividing the launch height by the time. You should find that any individual glider has about the same sink rate no matter from what height you launch it.

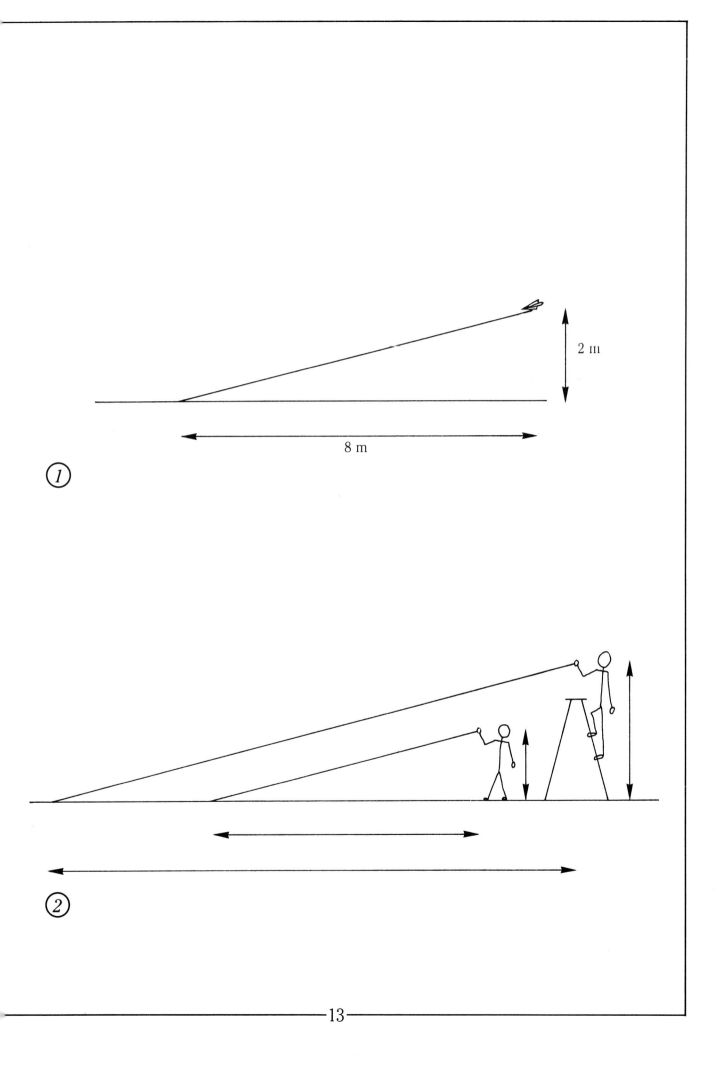

2 m

8 m

①

②

6
BASIC FORM

The next few designs owe something to origami, the Japanese art of paper folding. They illustrate some of the many shapes that can be made from a single sheet of paper, and may help you to create particular forms when you come to design your own paper planes. They all start with this basic form.

You will need:
1 A4 sheet of paper

When you make these designs, do not forget to trim them, and measure their glide ratios and sink rates, to compare them with the darts you made earlier. Do not feel confined by the designs as shown: try making wings bigger or smaller, or altering the sizes or angles of the keel and tip plates, test flying as you go along. If you do this carefully, and write down the results for each design, you will start to see how different shapes effect the flying performances of different designs.

Here's how to build it

Step 1   Fold a top corner of the paper down diagonally so that the short edge meets the long edge.

Step 2   Fold the right-hand flap towards you and bring it over to meet the left-hand edge. Fold the triangular top corner away from you, along the dashed line shown.

Step 3   Your piece of paper should now look like this.

Step 4   Open out the fold nearest to you to end up with this shape. Grip the three undermost layers of paper at point A, allowing the top layer of paper (B) to be taken over to meet point C.

Step 5   Before the folds are flattened, the paper should look like this.

Step 6   Flatten the folds to the finished basic form as shown here, taking care to ensure that the peak fold at B extends all the way to the corner.

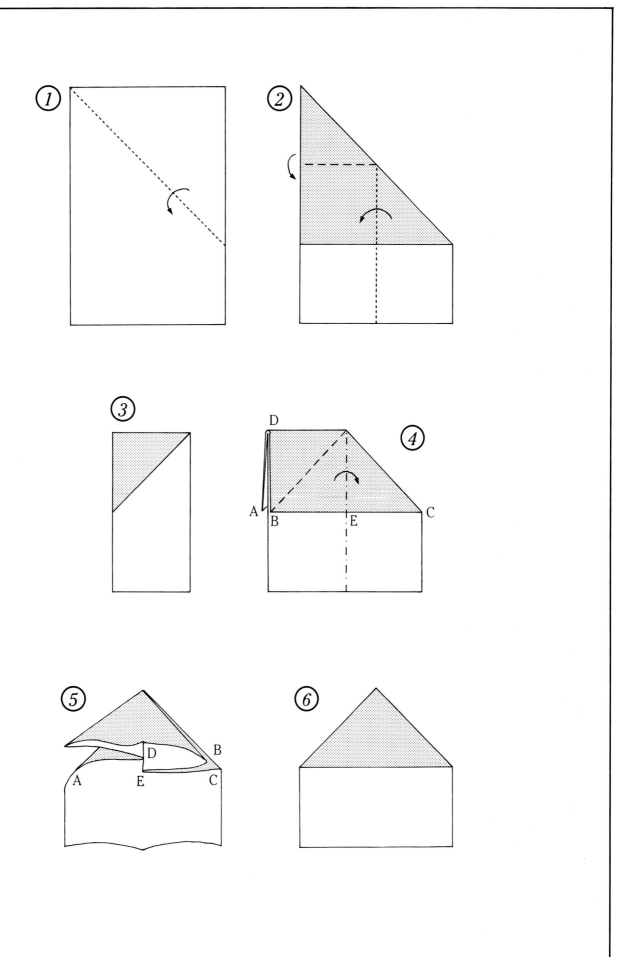

7
THE COCKPIT

If you look at any paper plane, you will notice that its weight is concentrated in front of the main part of its wings. We will look more closely at the effects of balance later on, but for now it is enough just to point out that this is to do with stability, and helps the glider to keep moving forward in much the same way as the concentration of a throwing dart's weight forward of its flights ensures that it can only fly in the forward direction. The cockpit of this design is not just for show; it also helps to keep the balance point, or centre of gravity, of this design well forward.

You will need:
1 A4 sheet of paper

Here's how to build it

Step 1   Begin with the Basic Form and fold the two triangular flaps along the dotted lines to meet on the vertical centre line.

Step 2   Fold these flaps in half again to form a kite shape.

Step 3   Fold inwards down the centre crease, bringing one half over to meet the other.

Step 4   Fold firstly along the dotted line, by opening out the wing nearest to you, then turn over and repeat the fold on the other wing. Next, fold the tip plates back towards the uppermost side of the wings on each side.

Step 5   Open out the plane to end up with the finished shape shown here.

You can show that it is not the actual position of the balance point that matters, but its position in relation to the working part of the wing. The tip plates determine how much wing area there is near the rear of the plane. If you make the tip plates too large, there will be less wing near the rear of the aeroplane and it will stall, while if you make the plates too small it will dive (try it and see).

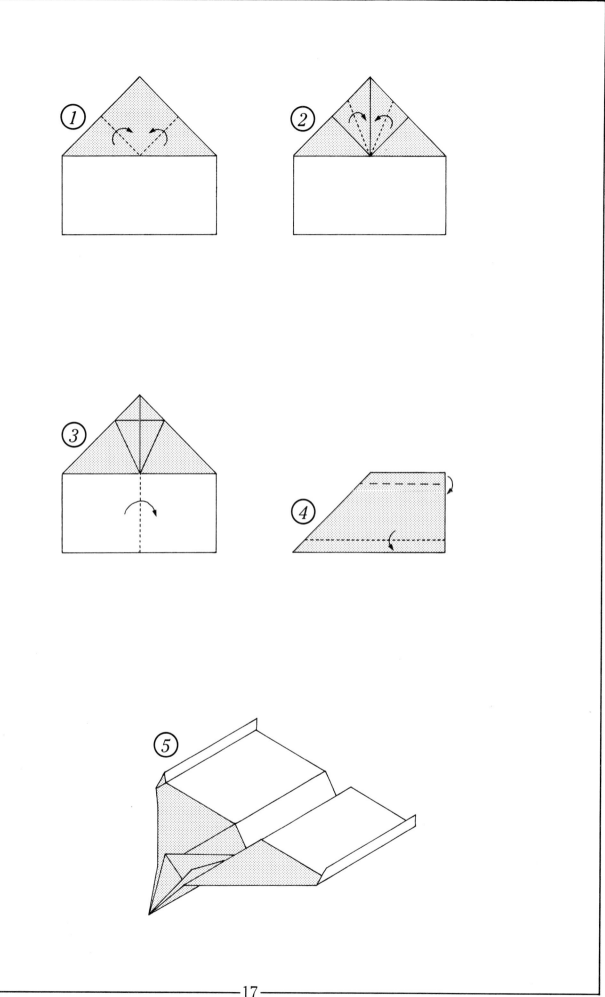

8

THE UNDERFOLD

This design is quite heavy for the size of its wings, and flies faster than the previous ones.

You will need:
1 A4 sheet of paper

Here's how to build it

Step 1   Begin with the Basic Form and fold the two triangular flaps upward to meet on the vertical centre line. Fold these flaps in half again but then open them out. (The creases formed are shown with dotted and dashed lines.)

Step 2   Fold the flaps in half the other way, bringing the top edge down to the centre line to create an upside-down kite shape. Once again open the flaps out, just leaving the creases.

Step 3   The folds in the previous steps have left a criss-cross pattern of creases to act as guides to the formation of the two points which will become the nose of the glider.

Step 4   Taking one of the criss-cross patterned flaps, fold both its short edges simultaneously towards the vertical centre line, causing a small peak in the centre of the flap which should be pinched together and folded forward towards the nose. Repeat for the other flap. Make a fold along the dashed line, folding away from you.

Step 5   This is the shape you will now have before you. Fold in half down the centre line.

Step 6   Turn the plane on its side as shown. Fold along the dotted line, opening the wings towards you. Turn over and repeat on the other side. Fold the paper along the dashed line towards the uppermost side of the wings, to make the tip plates.

Step 7   Open out as shown.

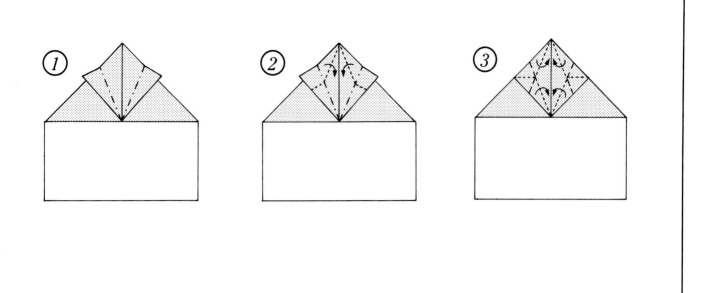

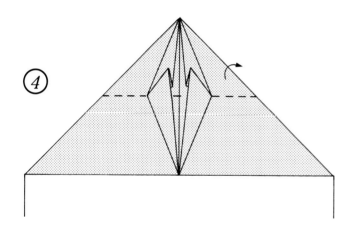

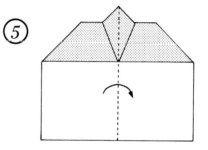

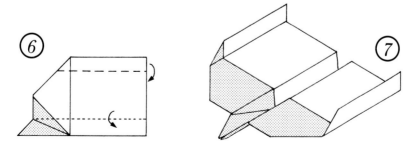

9
THE DONKEY

The underfold can be modified to investigate what happens when we put a tail on a paper aeroplane.

You will need:

1 A4 sheet of paper, scissors

Here's how to build it

Step 1   Divide the sheet of paper into a square and a rectangle by cutting off the excess formed after folding down the top right-hand corner diagonally towards you to meet the long edge.

Step 2   Fold the top triangle away from you and the other triangle in towards the middle and then open this second flap out.

Step 3   Hold the three undermost layers of paper at point A, allowing the top layer of paper (B) to be taken over to meet point C.

Step 4   Before the folds are flattened, your 'square' should look like this.

Step 5   Proceed as for The Underfold steps 1 to 4, then turn your 'triangle' over to look like this.

Step 6   Fold the rectangle of excess paper (from Step 1) lengthwise down the middle and cut to the size and shape shown. Use the diagram as a template. Fold down the flaps along the dotted line, one each side.

Step 7   Join the tail to the wings by inserting it under the flap indicated.

Step 8   Your finished plane will look like this.

In practice, the flexibility of the paper that supports the tail makes a tailed plane difficult to trim for straight flight. If you see any competition planes with tails, you will probably find that they have been strengthened by card or lamination.

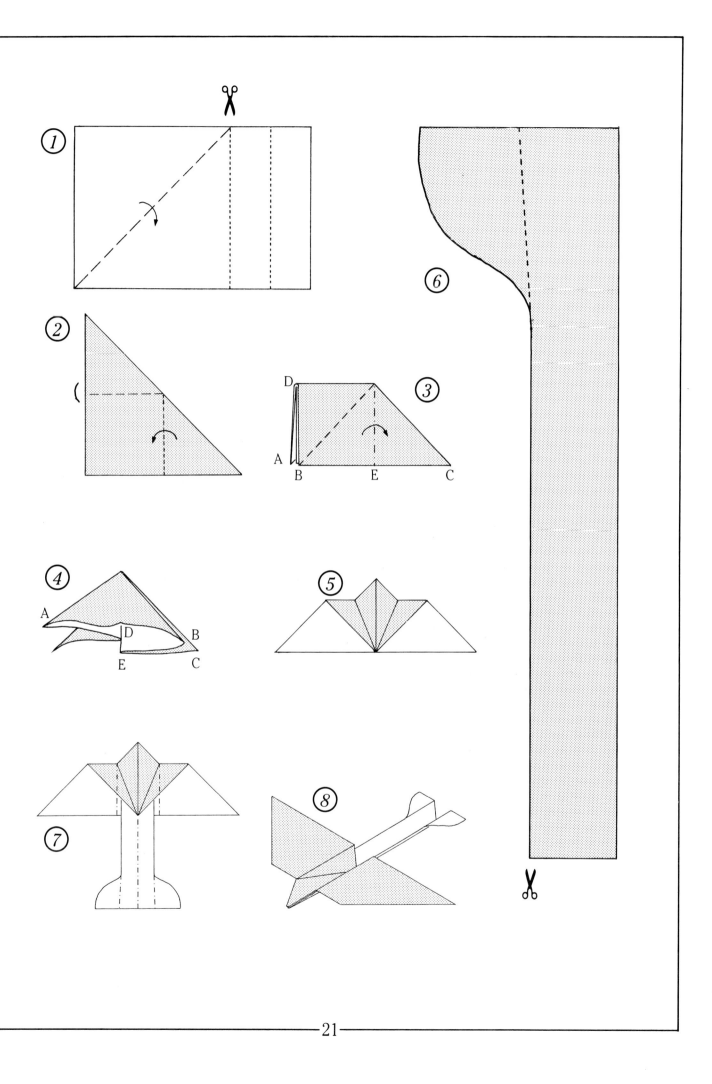

10
THE BOMBER

The bomber is also based on the basic form but is made upside-down in comparison with the other designs.

You will need:
1 A4 sheet of paper

Here's how to build it

Step 1   Begin with Basic Form, then lift the two triangular flaps upwards so that they come together.

Step 2   Fold the bottom half of the basic form in the opposite direction, until the two halves meet.

Step 3   Fold along the dotted line bringing the triangular flap towards the centre line.

Step 4   Fold the flap in half again.

Step 5   Fold in half once more.

Step 6   Repeat steps 3, 4 and 5 on the other side. To form the wings, fold along the dotted line, bringing the wing towards you. Repeat on the other side.

Step 7   Notice that the wings overlap the keel a little.

Step 8   Your finished plane should look like this. The protruding flaps form what (with a little imagination!) resembles an underslung bomb load.

The 'bombs' put the centre of gravity of this design quite low in relation to the wings. You may notice that this makes the bomber fly more upright, and therefore straighter than the previous designs. It also tends to dive, so trim (as for short dart type B, page 8) by bending the trailing edges of the wing upwards. Notice that the wings are somewhat flexible because of the arrangement of layers of paper below the glider rather than above as in the cockpit, reducing the glide angle achieved. It is interesting how such seemingly trivial differences in design can have noticeable effects on performance.

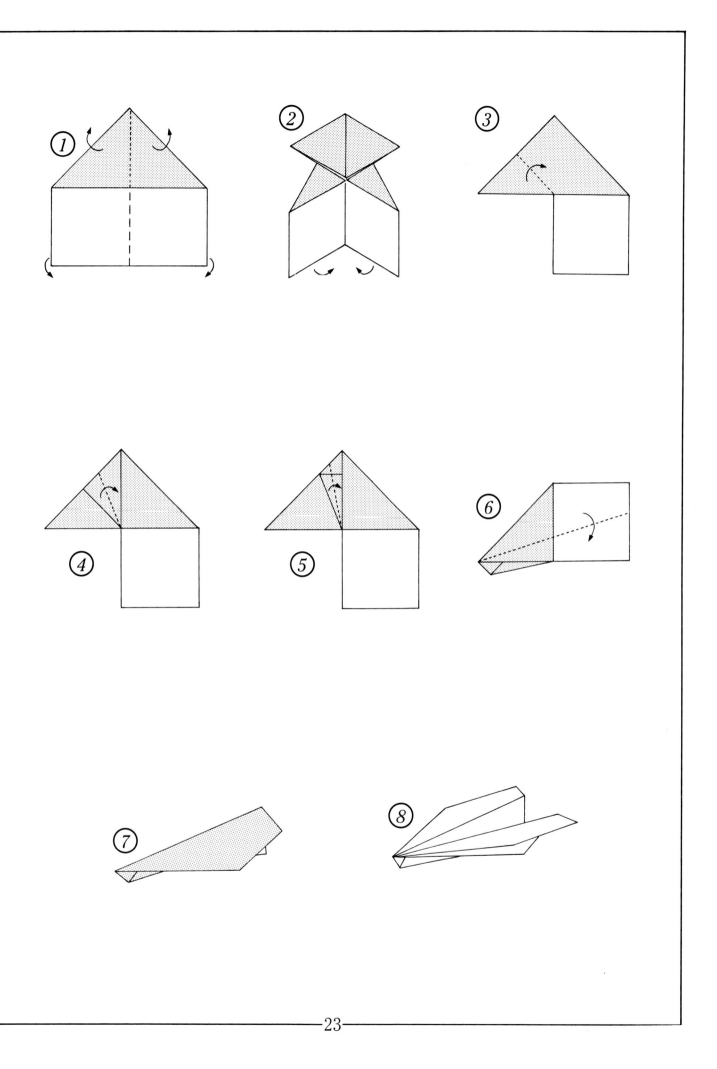

11
THE HEADSCARF

This rather odd flying object shows how effective a simple, strong design can be, even if it bears no resemblance to a full-size aeroplane. Its curved wing is quite rigid in the longitudinal direction (from the circular rim to the point).

You will need:
1 A4 sheet of paper, scissors

Here's how to build it

Step 1   Cut a piece of A4 paper along the dotted line to produce a right-angled triangular sheet.

Step 2   Fold in the long edge three times.

Step 3   The diagram shows the result of step 2.

Step 4   Tuck the tips into each other to form the headscarf shape.

To fly, hold the headscarf by its point, with the rim facing away from you, and launch it gently and smoothly straight ahead. The curved 'wing' of the headscarf makes it fly very reliably, but it is difficult to trim to fly any differently from the way it wants to. If you find out how to trim it to turn reliably, write and tell me about it!

Even though it looks odd, notice that it does share various features with the darts — its wing is stiffened by folds, and it has its weight quite far forward. The curve in the wing also gives a dihedral effect.

If you have read through the book until this point without making any of the designs or doing any of the experiments, why not have a go now? It will help you make the most of the rest of the book. On the other hand, if you have been building and flying as you go along, you will have gained the experience needed to fully appreciate the rather special design that comes next.

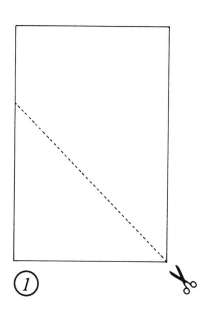

①

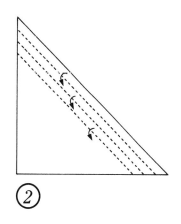

②

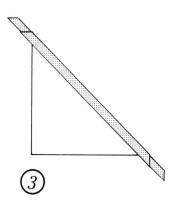

③

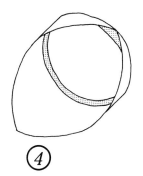

④

12
THE PAPERANG

Now that you have had some practice at making and flying paper aeroplanes, it is time to look at one which has been designed to fly really well, and yet is still easy to build.

You will need:
1 A4 sheet of paper, scissors and a stapler

Here's how to build it

Step 1   Fold the paper in half widthways.

Step 2   Fold the corner back along the dotted line on both sides.

Step 3   Your piece of paper should now look like this. The dotted line indicates the next fold.

Step 4   Fold the flaps forward on both sides along the dotted line shown in the previous diagram, and make the cut indicated.

Step 5   The dotted line indicates the next fold.

Step 6   Fold back the flap on the side facing you.

Step 7   Fold the flap again, along the dotted line shown in the previous diagram. Now repeat this and the previous step for the other side.

Step 8   Hold the leading edges and the two wing tips exactly together and use scissors to cut out the trailing edge shape shown full-size in the diagram. (Cut from the top downwards towards the middle crease, to make both wings exactly the same shape). The cut can be made by eye, or you can trace the full-sized outline given here.

Step 9   Fold the small flap (indicated by the dotted line) on the side facing you.

Step 10   Open up the paperang along the middle crease, allowing the unfolded small flap from the opposite side to lie on top of the folded flap of step 9.

Step 11   Fold the second flap back and under the first flap along the dashed line indicated in the previous diagram. Check that all the folds are well flattened. Hold the paperang centrally in the jaws of a stapler so that the staple will come right through the paperang to the underside of the wing. Ensure that all the folds are in place, and then staple.

Step 12   Bend the staple to give the wings a slight amount of dihedral or upsweep. Hold the paperang so that it points directly away from you. Look along the middle fold and compare the curve of the two wings. It is important that there is the same amount of arch or billow in both wings. If one billows more than the other, it can be evened out by gently but firmly sliding the top surface under the staple towards the flatter side. (It sounds difficult, but you only need to move the top surface very slightly for the billow to alter a lot).

Step 13   The paperang is now ready for test flying.

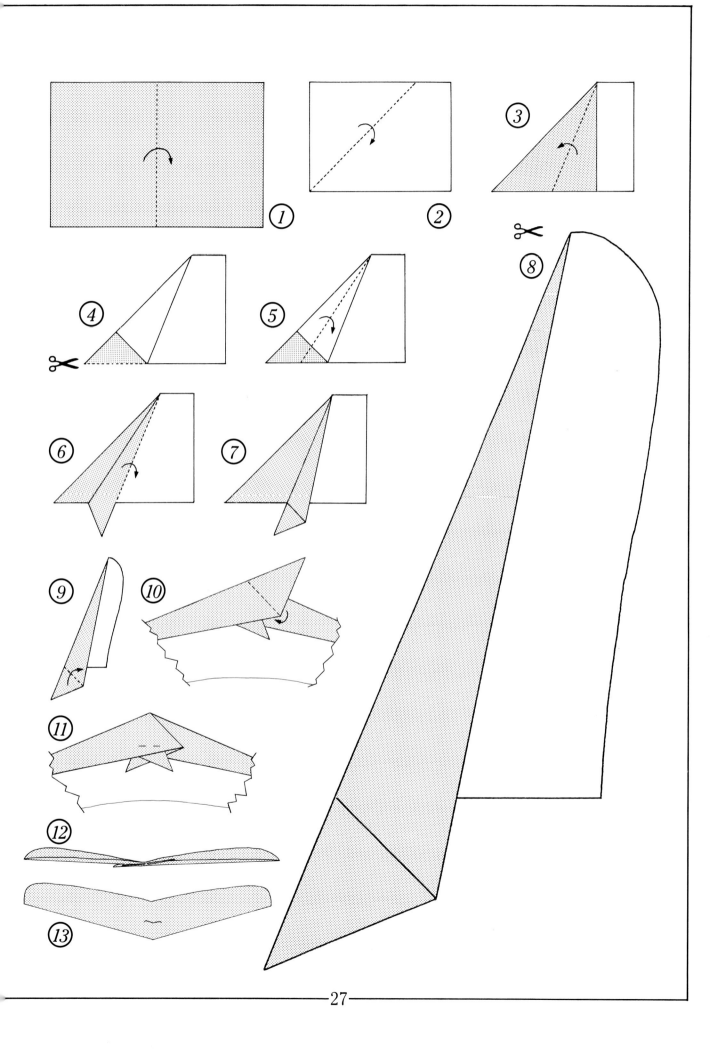

FLYING THE PAPERANG

The long, thin wings of the paperang allow it to fly much further than other paper aeroplanes, but it requires careful launching because there is no keel for you to hold.

Handle the paperang by its strong centre section only. For the first flights, use a large draught-free indoor space such as a school gym. The paperang has a glide ratio of at least 8, so from a shoulder-high launch you can expect a 10-15 m flight when properly trimmed.

Launch
Hold the paperang with the nose slightly down and with the wings level (Figure 1). Launch it fairly fast, releasing it cleanly. If you open your thumb and finger wide as you release it, you will avoid brushing the paperang and slowing it down (Figure 2).

The goal is to launch it at its natural flying speed, which you will be able to judge after a few tries. If you have built it accurately, it will fly in a beautifully straight line, to come to a sliding stop more than 10 m away (about double the distance that a paper dart would fly if launched from the same height). If it does not do this, it should be trimmed.

Trimming
Look carefully at the paperang to check that the wings are symmetrical. If the paperang is turning during the flight but you cannot see why, gently slide the top surface of the wing under the staple, increasing the billow of wing on the outside of the turn.

Figure 3 shows a paperang that tends to turn to the left because the left wing has more billow. To rectify this, the paperang can be trimmed by moving the top surface to the right. If you have difficulty and the paperang turns in opposite directions even after successive adjustments, bend the staple a little more to increase the dihedral.

If the paperang glides straight ahead but dives to the ground, bend the last 1 cm of both wing tips slightly upwards (Figure 4). If it stalls, the easiest solution is to add a small piece of Blu-Tack to the nose.

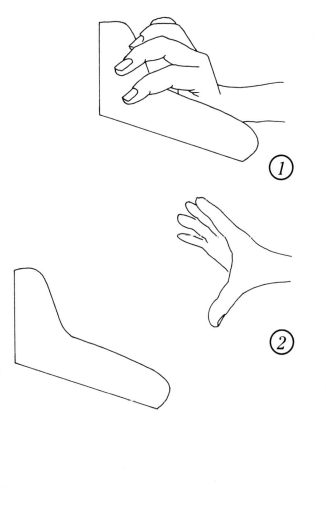

①

②

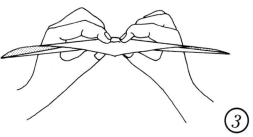

③

④

14
PERFORMANCE MEASUREMENT II

The versatile paperang can be modified to produce improved glide ratio or sink rate, but measuring these improvements requires a little thought.

Figure 1   Sink rate is calculated as with the darts, but you may find that glide ratio is more difficult, since the paperang tends to level out before landing. This 'ground effect' is due to a layer of air trapped between the wings and the ground. It appears when the glider comes to within half a wing span of the ground. The paperang is cushioned more than other paper planes because it has no keel. The error will be similar for all launches from a given height, however, so the calculated glide ratios will be useful for comparisons between paperangs, even if they are not absolutely accurate when comparing paperangs with darts.

Figure 2   The distance a glider flies will also depend on how hard you throw it. Anyone who has thrown a ball will be familiar with the flight path it takes, slowing down as it flies upwards and speeding up as it comes back down again. This is called the ballistic flight path, named after the ballista, an ancient cannon.

Figure 3   The distance travelled on a ballastic flight, as well as the duration of the flight, depends on the speed and angle of the launch, not on lift from the wings. This contrasts with the normal flight of a glider, which is intimately related to the performance of the wings. Competitions often allow ballistic launches, in which the glider is launched at an angle upwards as hard as possible. As the glider gains height and slows down to a speed approaching its natural flying speed it should begin to glide at a steady speed. A ballistic launch basically converts launch speed into extra height, allowing the glider to fly further and for longer than it would if it were launched at its natural flying speed.

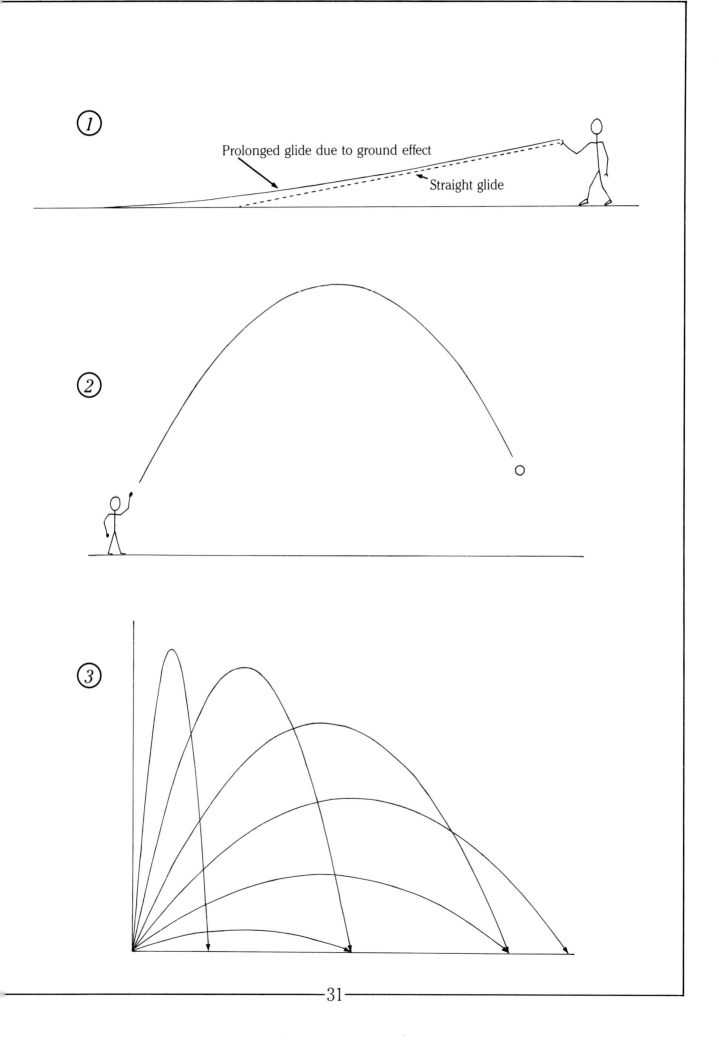

15
ENTERING COMPETITIONS

The paperang will win competitions, particularly when the rules favour good natural glide angle or sink rate, although its advantage of quick assembly from a single piece of A4 paper and a staple are seldom rewarded.

Distance competitions are usually decided by the length of the straight line from the launch point to touchdown (Figure 1). This means that you must be certain that your entry is well trimmed to fly straight, which in any case is a good idea because it will always fly more efficiently in a straight line. Your glider might fly a circle with a 10 m diameter, but if it lands at your feet you will score zero!

Some distance competitions allow ballistic launches and are decided simply on the furthest distance reached, in the manner of a javelin competition. In these, the ability of the glider to travel in a straight line when thrown as hard as possible becomes the most important flight characteristic. The gliding phase need only be employed if it would increase the distance flown.

Figure 2 shows the flight paths of gliders employing only ballistic phases and of those employing both ballistic and gliding phases. The distance achieved on a ballistic path can only be bettered if the glider can commence gliding sometime after reaching the top of the flight. The paperang is not very suitable for such competitions. Since wings not only introduce the possibility of veering off course during the ballistic phase, but also increase drag throughout the flight and therefore decrease the maximum height (and therefore distance) attained, it is very difficult to improve on the performance of long, thin dart shapes that are strong enough to fly straight when thrown as hard as possible.

Figure 3 shows a contest-winning dart that you may like to try. Fold the paper in half lengthways, and then fold the two sides in so that the long edges of the paper meet along the centre fold. Fold one corner down to make a right-angled triangle, then keep folding the wing towards you, always keeping the bottom line horizontal, until four folds have been completed. Repeat for the other side. This dart will fly very straight no matter how hard you throw it.

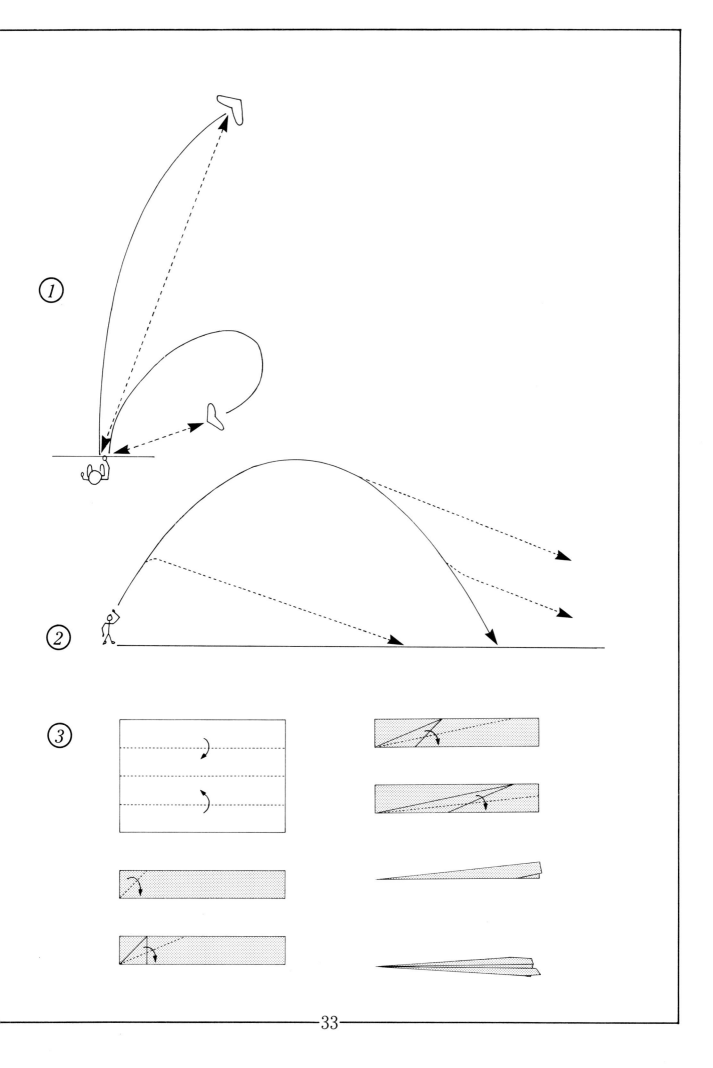

16
TIME IN THE AIR

The paperang is particularly suited to time in the air competitions where duration is measured from a launch at flying speed.

Launch 1 If ballistic launches are allowed, a little thought and practice will be required. Since the ballistic part of the flight is at high speed and contributes little to the flight time, the launch is best used to propel the glider upwards as high as possible, from which point it can return slowly to the ground. The glider has to have low drag and high stability during the ballistic phase in order to achieve the best height, yet it must also be trimmed for the gliding part of the flight. Wing stiffness is critical, since a slight bend which would only slightly affect the plane's performance during the gliding phase can cause a loop during the ballistic phase. If you use a paperang for ballistic-launched duration competitions, you will find that the less washout it has, the greater the height it will achieve when in the ballistic phase of the launch.

Launch 2 The paperang has a tendency to loop when launched hard and it turns out that the best ballistic strategy is to launch it horizontally just hard enough for it to reach the top of the loop, and then stall in the inverted position and recover into a gliding flight.

Launched correctly, paperangs can achieve heights of 10 m or so, for durations of around 10 seconds. The Racer (no 19, page 40) is the best variant to try — it has the strongest wings, low drag, low washout and high natural flying speed. If you want to improve on this, you might try experimenting with a racer mounted on a tailed fuselage made from stiff card or laminated paper. The centre of gravity of such a design needs to be quite far forward and will need some Blu-Tack on the nose.

AEROBATICS

Turn

This can be achieved whenever a paperang is launched with the wings banked. The more steeply the wings are inclined, the tighter the turn will be.

If launched at normal gliding speed, the paperang will turn while slowly levelling out (Figure 1). If launched hard, it may circle up to three times before landing. You will be able to get your paperang to come back to your hand with a little practice (like a non-spinning paper boomerang, hence the name). If launched slightly upwards with slightly banked wings, the paperang will perform a stall turn: climbing in a near straight line while slowing to a stop, it will then pivot on a wing-tip before diving back down on a near straight return path (Figure 2).

Loop

Launch the paperang upwards hard in front of you, using a pulling grip as shown in Figure 3.

Touch and go

Launch quite hard towards a polished floor with wing-tips level, and nose down at an angle a little steeper than its natural glide angle (Figure 4).

Lomcevac

This manoeuvre is more random than the accurately defined spin and tumble performed by aerobatic display pilots but, on occasion, the paperang does go through a complex flight path that comes close to a real lomcevac.

Hold the paperang by the tip of one spar and give a frisbee-like upward launch (Figure 5). It will continue for a revolution or two, and then recover violently, possibly turning upside down before going into a vertical dive, then pulling out into a straight glide again. This is unique to the paperang, since other paper planes have large stabilizing surfaces which prevent them being launched into a spin.

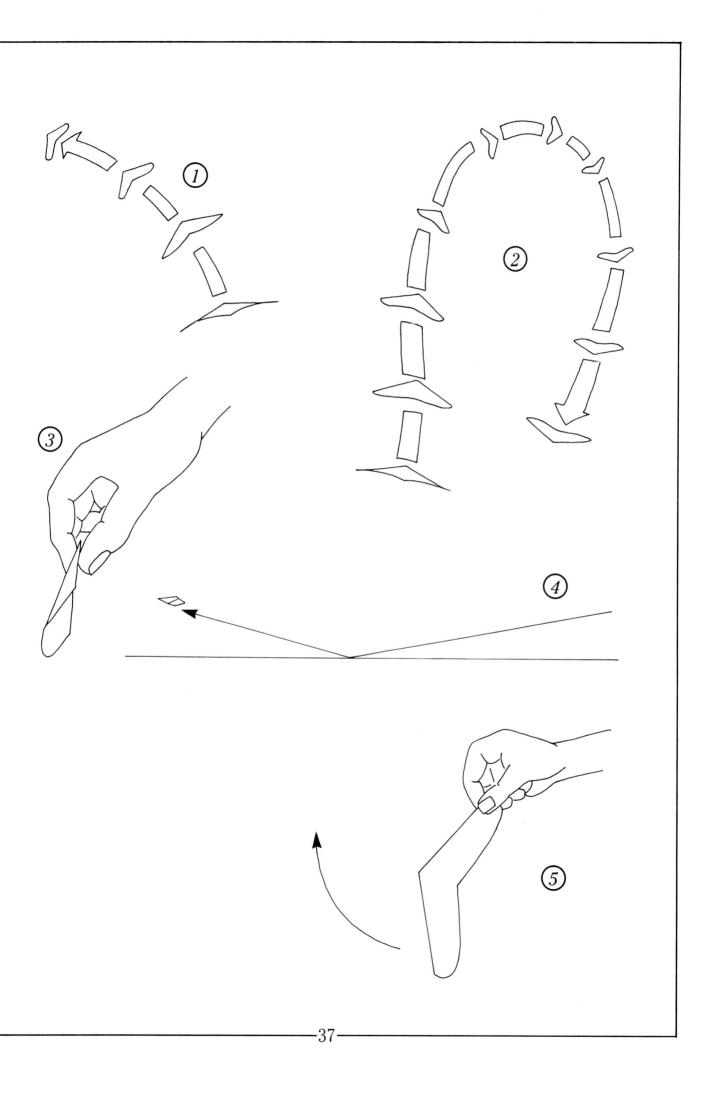

THE FLOATER

The floater has thinner, lighter spars as well as larger wings with more swept-back leading edges than the standard paperang. The sweepback of the wings is increased by making the central cut shorter than the standard paperang. These modifications lower its flying speed, and make it more stable. It has an impressively slow, flat glide.

You will need:
1 A4 sheet of paper, scissors and a stapler

Here's how to build it

Step 1   Fold the paper in half as shown.

Step 2   Fold the corner back along the dotted line, on both sides.

Step 3   Measure 55 mm along the bottom left-hand edge and make a cut as indicated. Fold from this point up to the corner shown by the dotted line. Now cut off this flap. Repeat on the other side.

Step 4   Fold the flap in half on itself and repeat on the other side.

Step 5   Fold the flap back, up to the end of the cut.

Step 6   Cut off the ends of the spars along the dotted line.

Step 7   Cut the trailing edge as shown in this template. Open out and staple through the spars as for the standard paperang.

You will notice that the floater is not as stiff as the standard paperang, and it does not automatically assume exactly the best shape for flying. The wings of the floater may need to have a little extra billow bent into them, otherwise the wing tips tend to be a little floppy. You can do this by bending the staple into a V-shape as before, and then increasing the billow in each wing by bringing the leading edges towards the keel. Do not bend the leading edges when you do this. Note that the wings are cone-shaped, the arch of the billow decreasing in span towards the nose (Figure 8); increase the billow to accentuate this cone shape. Trimming for turns cannot be carried out as in the standard paperang, by sliding the top surface under the staple, because of the forward position of the staple. Instead, trimming should be performed by bending the whole of the glider to even out the billows of the two wings.

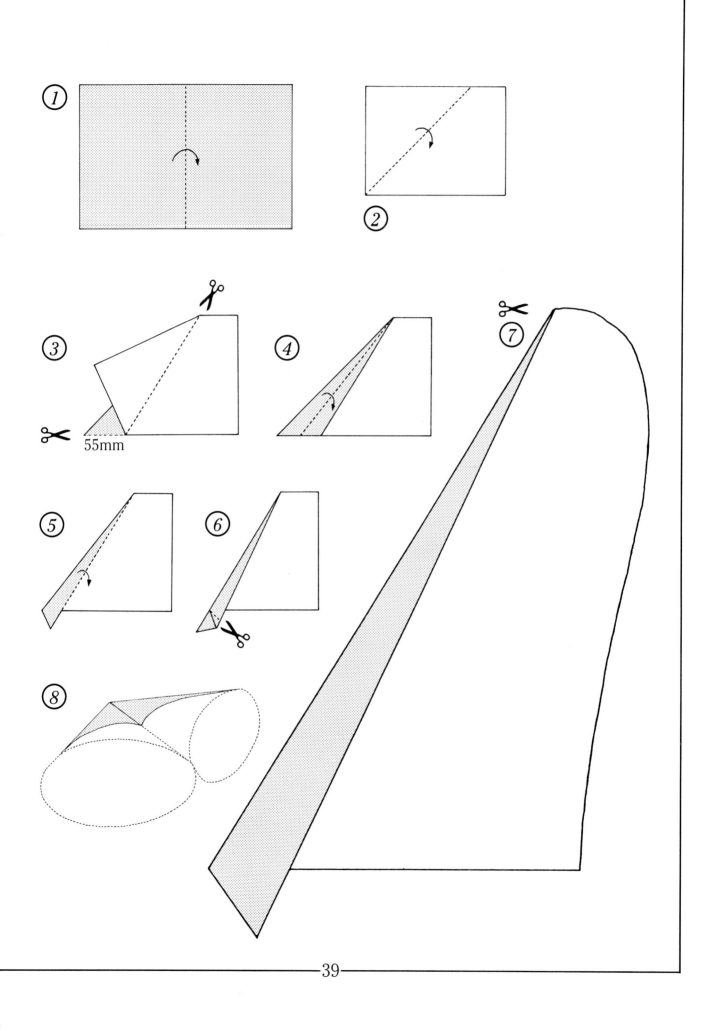

55mm

19
THE RACER

The cut of the trailing edge gives the racer narrower wings than the standard paperang, while its spars are glued to the undersurface of its wings. These modifications combine to give a plane which flies fast and can be launched hard.

You will need:
1 A4 sheet of paper, scissors and Pritt or similar dry glue and a stapler

Here's how to build it

Step 1   Fold the paper in half widthways.

Step 2   Fold the corner back along the dotted line, on both sides.

Step 3   Your piece of paper should now look like this. The dotted line indicates the next fold.

Step 4   Fold flaps forward on both sides, along the dotted line shown in the previous diagram, and make the cut indicated.

Step 5   The dotted line indicates the next fold.

Step 6   Fold the flap back on the side facing you, along the line shown in the previous diagram.

Step 7   Fold the flap again along the dotted line shown in the previous diagram. Now repeat this and the previous step for the other side. Cut the wing-tips off as indicated.

Step 8   Hold the leading edges and the two wing-tips exactly together and use scissors to cut out the trailing edge shape shown in the actual size diagram. Cut from the top downwards towards the middle crease, to make both wings exactly the same shape.

Step 9   Unfold the last fold of the spars and apply Pritt or similar dry glue to the surface that will come into contact with the upper surface of the wing.

Step 10   Refold the spar carefully, sticking it to the underside of the wing, then staple as with the paperang.

When complete, check the surfaces are in alignment as before. The wings are very narrow, and there is little or no washout. Washout can be increased if necessary either by twisting the spars gently, by bending the tips of the spars upwards as described for the standard paperang, or by increasing the billow as was described for the floater. Trim to correct turning by increasing the washout in the wing on the outside of the turn using any of these methods.

 You will find that the lower drag of this design allows it to fly both faster and with a flatter glide than the standard paperang. Once you have trimmed the Racer to fly straight and level, try holding it in the pulling grip (Figure 11) and launch it vertically upwards as hard as you can. If made accurately, the racer will perform multiple loops.

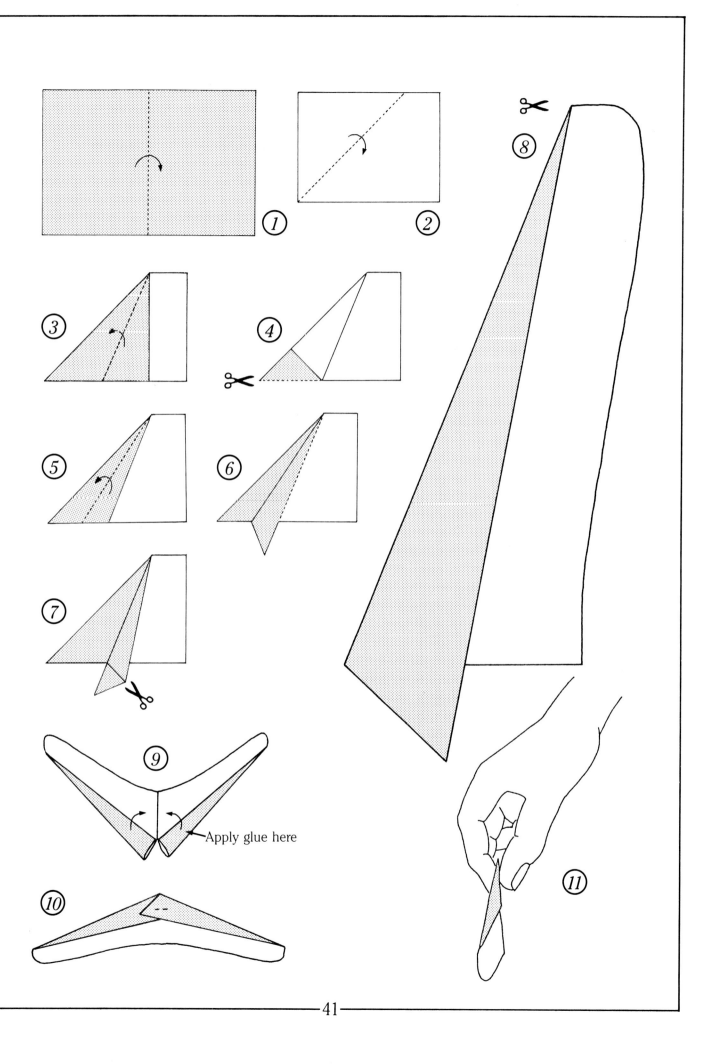

Apply glue here

20
THE THEORY OF FLYING

What makes a paper aeroplane fly rather than drop to the ground like a stone? The following pages provide an introduction to the answer to that question.

Newton's laws state that a body moving in a straight line at a steady speed will continue to do so, as long as there are no resultant forces acting on it. For instance, a spaceship travelling outside the pull of gravity has no forces whatsoever acting on it (Figure 1), while in a powered aircraft all forces acting on it cancel each other out (Figure 2).

The forces acting on a gliding paper plane are its weight and the total aerodynamic reaction (R for short). The weight of the glider acts vertically downwards and is dependent only on the mass of the glider. R is the total of all the forces arising from the movement of the glider through the air and, in a glider travelling in a straight line at a steady speed, R equals the weight and acts vertically upwards. Weight and R are represented in the diagram (Figure 3) by arrows (vectors) whose directions are the same as the directions of the forces, and whose lengths represent the size of those forces.

In vector diagrams the geometric relationships between the vectors of known forces can be used to calculate forces that are difficult or impossible to measure directly. In the diagram the central point corresponds to the centre of gravity of the glider (which has been omitted to keep the diagram simple). R is made up of two component forces. One of these forces is drag, defined as the total of all the forces that act in the direction opposite to that of the motion of the glider. The second component is lift, which is defined as the force acting at right angles to drag.

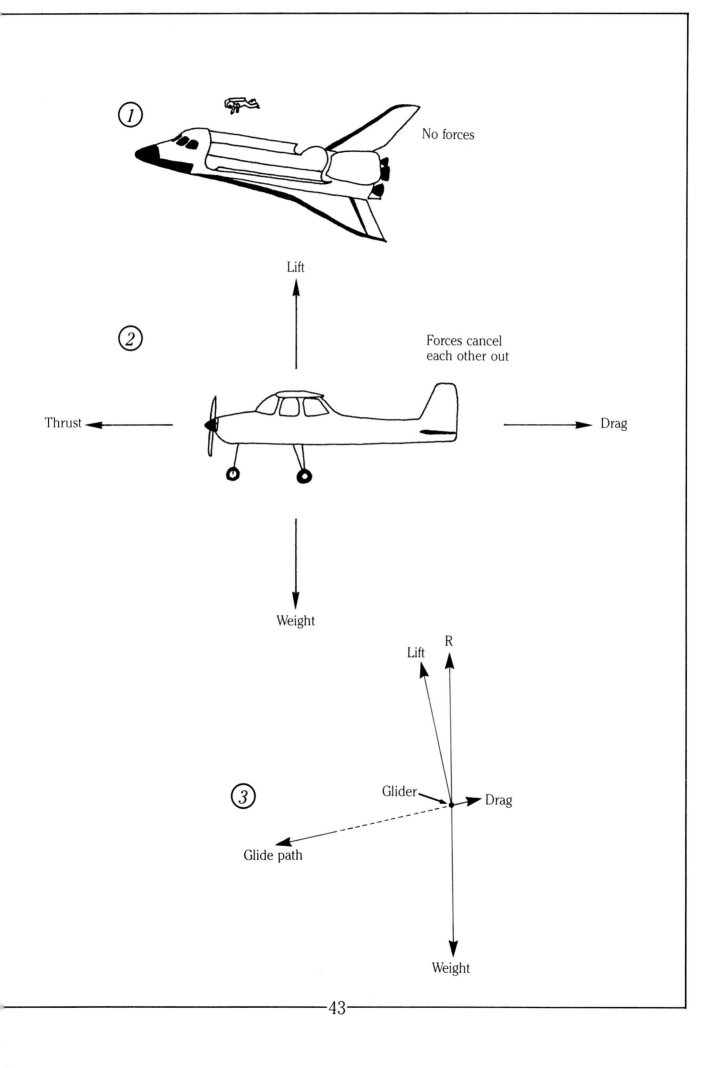

① No forces

② Forces cancel each other out

Lift

Thrust

Drag

Weight

③ R

Lift

Glider — Drag

Glide path

Weight

21
LIFT AND DRAG

Lift
Lift is produced when the air passing over the top surface of the wing is at a lower pressure than the air passing under the bottom surface. This is achieved by giving the wing an airfoil cross-section, and by inclining it upwards to the airflow.

Drag
Drag arises from the friction between the plane's surfaces and the airflow (form drag), as well as from the production of lift (induced drag). Induced drag is the result of vortices at the wing-tips formed when air flows away from the high pressure below the wing towards the low pressure above the wing. This is shown in Figure 1.

Lift:drag ratio
Figure 2 shows the geometrical relationships of the forces shown in Figure 3, page 43. Those of you who are familiar with vector addition will see that, given that lift acts at right angles to the direction of motion and that drag acts opposite to the direction of motion, the glide ratio will be defined by the ratio of lift to drag. We have already used glide ratio as a measure of a glider's performance and have calculated it from launch height and horizontal distance travelled. The fact that the glide ratio is the same as the lift:drag ratio is very useful; it tells us that if we can either increase the lift or decrease the drag acting on a glider, it will fly further from a given launch height.

Weight
The total aerodynamic reaction, R, must be equal and opposite to weight if a glider is to fly in a straight line at a steady speed. If you increase the weight of a glider, you will find its flying speed increases until the lift and drag generated balance the new weight. Thus, for a given wing area, the heavier a glider, the faster it will fly.

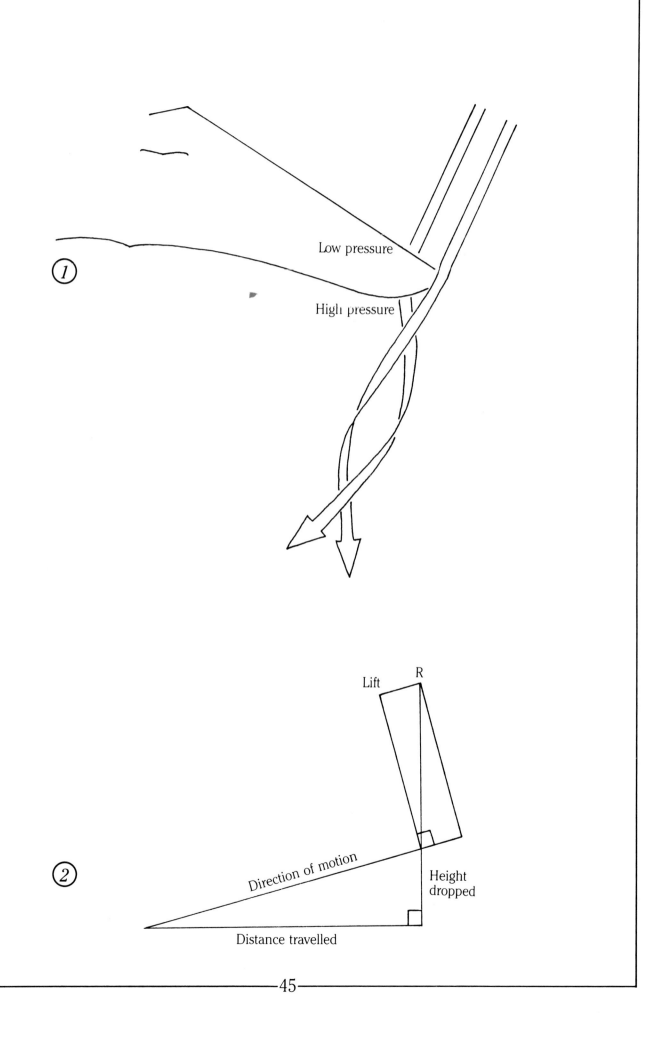

①

Low pressure

High pressure

②

Lift

R

Direction of motion

Height dropped

Distance travelled

22
STALLING

Stalling, the cause of the roller-coaster path that you have already come across, is an effect that causes sudden loss of control and height in all aircraft. An understanding of its causes will help you when you design your own paper aeroplanes.

The angle at which a wing is inclined to the airflow is called the angle of attack and is shown in Figure 1. The amount of lift produced by a wing depends both on the airspeed and on the angle of attack. Figure 2 shows a graph of the lift produced for various angles of attack by a wing at a given airspeed. At the stall angle, lift decreases suddenly whereas the amount of drag increases suddenly. Thus, when the wing of a glider reaches its stall angle in flight, the glider is slowed down suddenly by the increased drag, and dives violently because of the loss of lift.

These observations explain the roller-coaster path of a stalling glider. As the nose of the glider goes up, so the angle of attack is increased until stall angle is reached. The glider stalls, lift is suddenly lost, and the glider falls through the air. As the glider falls, it picks up speed, and if the flying surfaces are properly designed (see the section on Stability, page 48) the nose drops, decreasing the angle of attack of the wings which start to generate lift again and pull the glider out of the dive. As the airflow over the wing surfaces returns to normal speed, the balance of forces on the wing returns to normal (in this case a nose-light trim), and the process is repeated.

Stalling in full-sized aircraft is every bit as abrupt as it is in paper aeroplanes, and the effects of stalling are catastrophic. The leading edge slats and trailing edge flaps of jet airliners (look for them next time you fly) are elaborate devices designed to enable them to fly at the very low speeds and high angles of attack required to get into and out of airports without stalling.

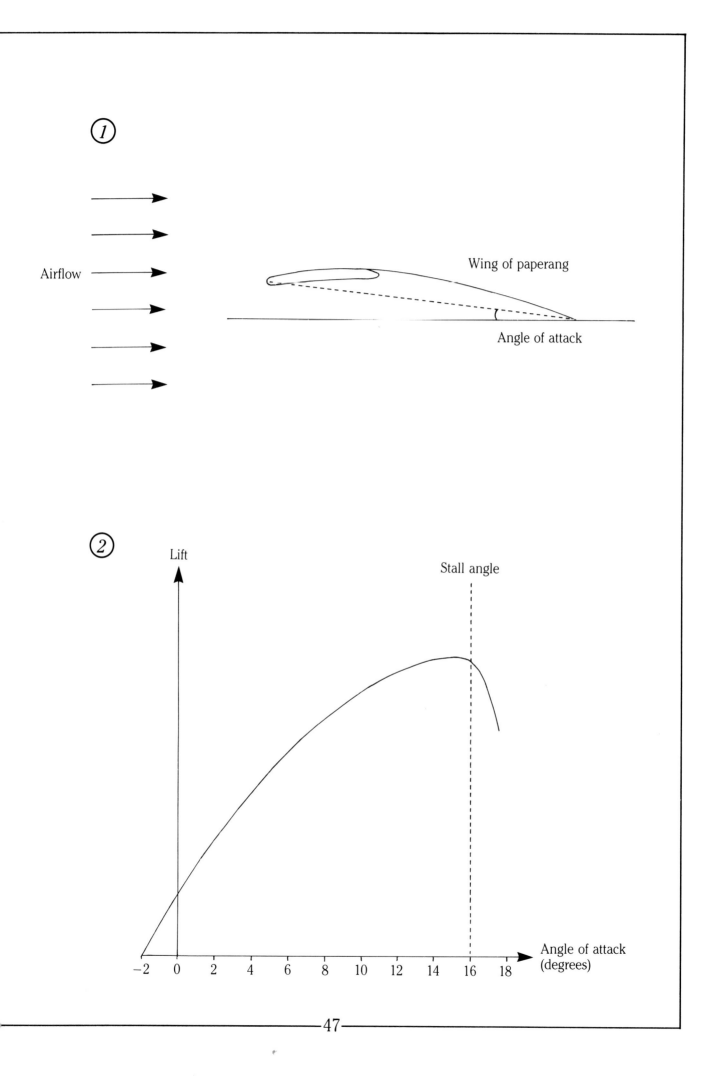

23
STABILITY

A glider in steady, straight-line flight will produce the balanced forces described in the last few pages. A glider is stable if it can return to such steady flight after a disturbance due to turbulence or gusts.

Attitude
The position of the glider in relation to the airflow is known as its attitude. Attitude can change by rotation around any of three axes as shown Figure 1. Rotation around the pitch axis refers to the nose-up and nose-down movements and is measured by the angle of attack of the wing. Rotation around the roll axis refers to banking movements, and around the yaw axis refers to flat turning movements (like a car skidding).

Pitch stability
On most full-sized aircraft, pitch stability is provided by surfaces at the tail called, very aptly, stabilizers. A simplified version of these stabilizers can be seen in Figure 2. Movements in the pitch axis caused by gusts or turbulence alter the angle of attack of the stabilizers which then produce a vertical force on the tail, returning the plane to its original attitude.

Yaw stability
Yaw stability is maintained in much the same way as pitch stability, with a vertical fin at the tail of the aircraft producing sideways forces to counteract yawing motions (Figure 2).

Roll stability
Stability in the roll axis is provided by dihedral, in two ways. Firstly, it tends to lower the centre of gravity, so that the weight of the glider itself tends to keep it upright. Secondly, wings produce maximum lift when horizontal, and progressively less when tilted, until they produce none at all when vertical. A pair of wings with dihedral which has been disturbed from the horizontal, such as in Figure 3, will produce more lift in the lower, more horizontal wing thus returning the glider to its original attitude on the roll axis.

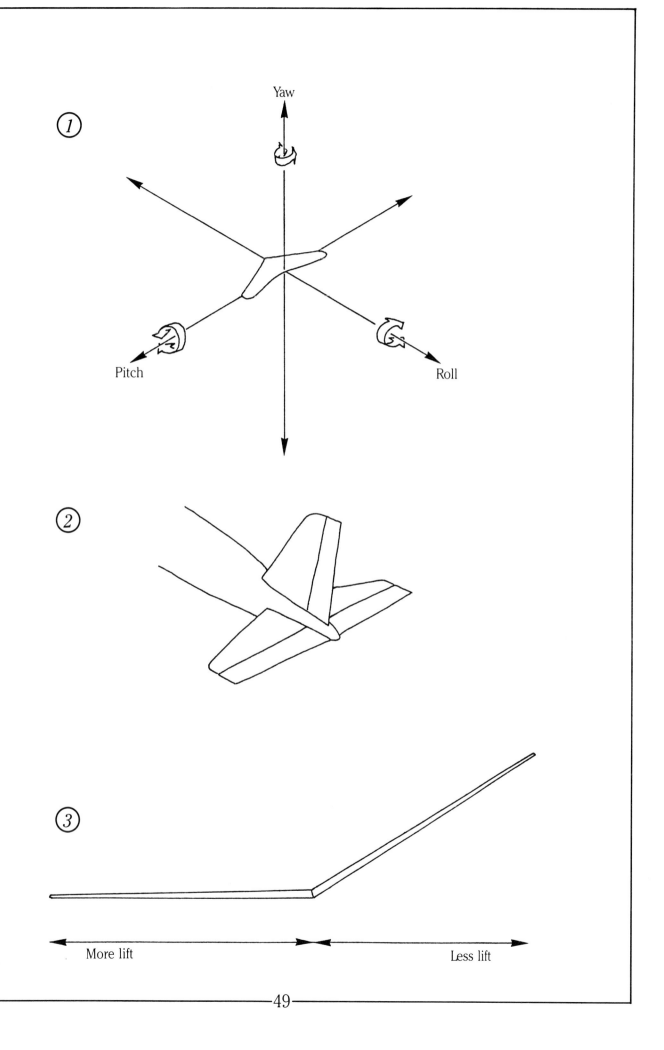

TRIMMING THE PAPERANG

Now that we have grappled with some aerodynamic theory, it is worth explaining the rather unusual way the basic paperang is trimmed.

If you try to bend the wings of the paperang as you might those of a dart, you will put unwanted warps into the rest of the wing. Also, the strengthening folds along the leading edge leave the wing weak along its chord, so if the trailing edge is bent upwards, the forces on this surface can bend the whole of the wing downwards, creating an effect opposite to the one desired, as in Figure 1.

A dive in the paperang is corrected by bending the tips of the spars upwards at right angles to the leading edge. This decreases the angle of attack and therefore the lift produced by the wing-tips. Because the wing-tips are at the rear of the glider the tail drops, correcting the dive. Pitching up is cured by adding weight to the nose of the glider, because it is difficult to reduce the washout by flattening the glider without destabilizing it.

The paperang has finely balanced yaw stability, which relies on accurate building rather than on vertical surfaces. Turns can be corrected while keeping roll and yaw in balance by increasing the billow of the wing on the outside of the turn, while flattening the billow on the inside. (This is the same system employed in hang gliders — Figure 2.) In order to correct a turn, you shift the top surface of the wing under the staple a little towards the outside of the turn, thus giving that side less lift and more drag. The staple holds the wing in the new position. This straightens out the unwanted turn with a co-ordinated effect on both the roll and yaw axes while retaining an efficient curve in the wing.

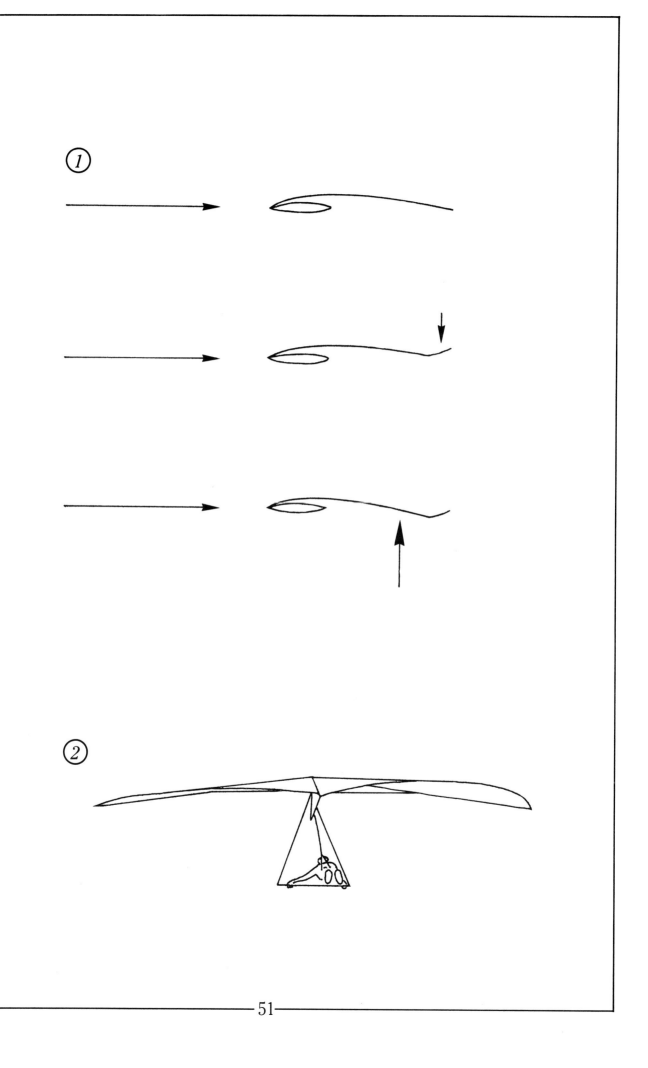

25
HIGH PERFORMANCE DESIGN

In engineering, if you want something strong, it will usually be heavy; if you want it light, it will usually be weak. If you want it both light and strong, it will very probably be expensive! Good design involves finding the best compromises: here are some that have been considered in designing the paperang.

Long, narrow (high aspect ratio) wings are more efficient than short fat ones. Aspect ratio is defined as the square of the wingspan divided by total wing area. All other factors being equal, the higher the aspect ratio, the higher the lift:drag ratio. Unfortunately, the longer the wings, the stiffer (and therefore heavier) they have to be. The paperang (Figure 1) has an aspect ratio of 7.4 compared with 1.6 for the short dart (Figure 2); but by careful design the paperang is stiffer, yet weighs less than a dart.

Figure 3 shows that if you examine a paperang from the side, you will see that the section at the wing-tip is twisted about 10° from the section at the centre. This washout prevents tip stalling, an undesirable condition in which a wing-tip stalls before the rest of the wing, causing the glider to turn unpredictably when it stalls. Tip stalls are prevented because the higher angle of attack at the centre of the wing means that the centre section stalls before the wingtips. In swept-back wings, washout also provides both pitch and yaw stability without the need for inefficient stabilizing surfaces. Unfortunately, washout reduces the efficiency of the wing, because each part of the wing works best at a certain angle of attack. Washout makes it impossible for all sections to be at their optimum angle at the same time. You will find that the less washout you build into a paperang, the more efficient it is, up to a point when it becomes unstable and unflyable.

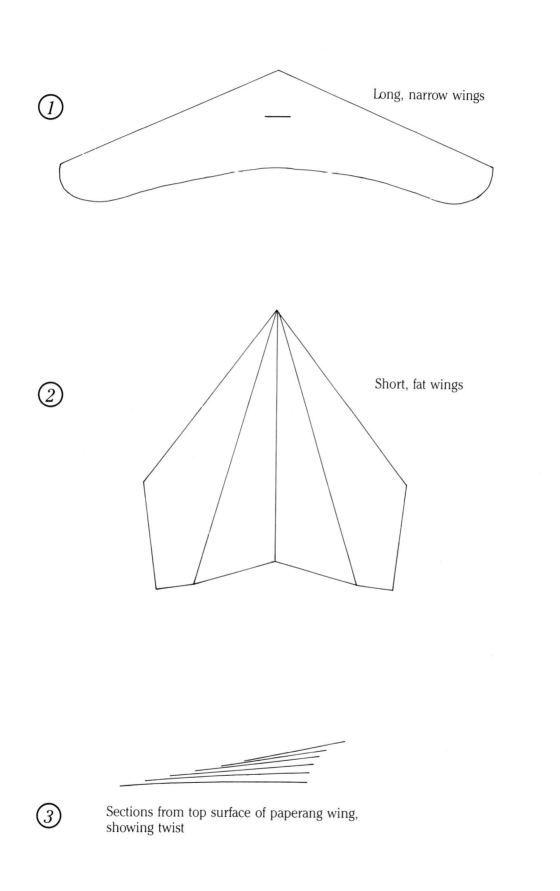

① Long, narrow wings

② Short, fat wings

③ Sections from top surface of paperang wing, showing twist

26
BALANCE

At the beginning of the book, you will have done experiments with the balance of the cockpit design. The following is a fuller explanation of those effects.

The weight of the glider acts on a point known as the balance point or centre of gravity (CG). The aerodynamic reaction, R, acts on a point, the centre of pressure (CP). The relative locations of these two points have a profound effect on the natural flying speed and stability of the glider. The further forward the CG, the faster and more stable the glider. If the CG is too far back, the glider becomes unflyable.

In flight, the position of the CG is fixed, whereas the CP changes with the attitude of the glider. The movement of the CP is determined by the design of the flying surfaces. The glider will be stable if the CP moves towards the rear in response to the glider pitching up, and towards the front if the glider dives. A well-trimmed paperang produces most of its lift at its centre section, and has its CG and CP located on the same vertical line (Figure 1). When the paperang pitches up, perhaps in response to a gust, the wing-tips start to produce lift (Figure 2) and move the CP rearwards. This has the stabilizing effect of pitching the paperang back towards level flight.

A piece of Blu-Tack added to the centre crease of the paperang at the trailing edge will move its CG rearwards (Figure 3). If the piece is large enough, you will find that no amount of trimming will enable the paperang to fly in a straight line at a steady speed. This is because even when the wing-tips produce lift (Figure 4), the CP will not move rearwards enough to stop the paperang from pitching up until it stalls.

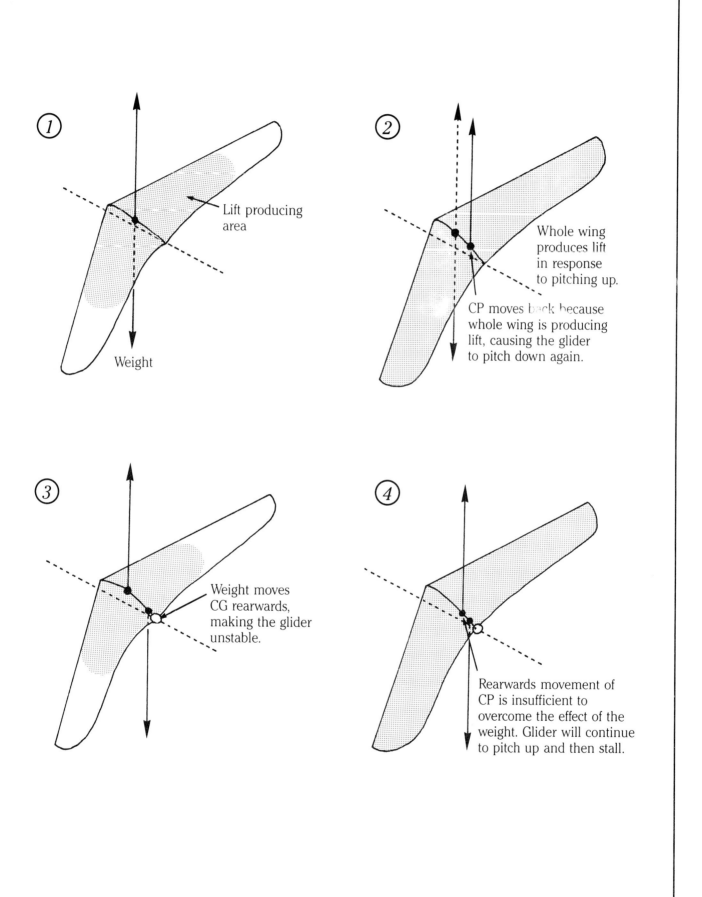

① Lift producing area

Weight

② Whole wing produces lift in response to pitching up.

CP moves back because whole wing is producing lift, causing the glider to pitch down again.

③ Weight moves CG rearwards, making the glider unstable.

④ Rearwards movement of CP is insufficient to overcome the effect of the weight. Glider will continue to pitch up and then stall.

DESIGNING PAPER AEROPLANES

Although standard aerodynamic theories apply to full-size aircraft as well as paper aeroplanes (Figure 1), standard aero-engineering does not, because of the limitations of paper as a structural material.

Paper planes are made by folding, limiting the shapes that are achievable, let alone airworthy. Paper is strengthened along folds, but weakened at right angles to them. It is difficult to arrange the folds so as to make paper planes sufficiently strong in all directions. Surfaces flex in flight, destroying accurate aerodynamic shapes. Most paper planes have poor flying performances because large proportions of their flying surfaces act as stabilizers to counteract the effects of flexing, adding to the planes' drag without producing useful lift. Also, most paper planes are so flexible that if they fly too fast, their flying surfaces distort so much that they become unstable and spiral into the ground (Figure 2). It follows that the first step in achieving a high performance paper aeroplane is to find a way to make it strong enough to keep an efficient aerodynamic shape in flight.

Any paper dart that has a V-shaped keel (Figure 3) has great longitudinal strength, but can only achieve a low gliding performance because the wings are not stiff and must be of low aspect ratio to stop them from flexing disastrously in flight. If paper is to be made into an aerodynamically efficient structure it must be supported, at least along its leading edge. Hang-gliders have simply-shaped flying surfaces made from sailcloth, supported at the leading edges by aluminium tubes. It was this basic similarity that led to the design of the paperang.

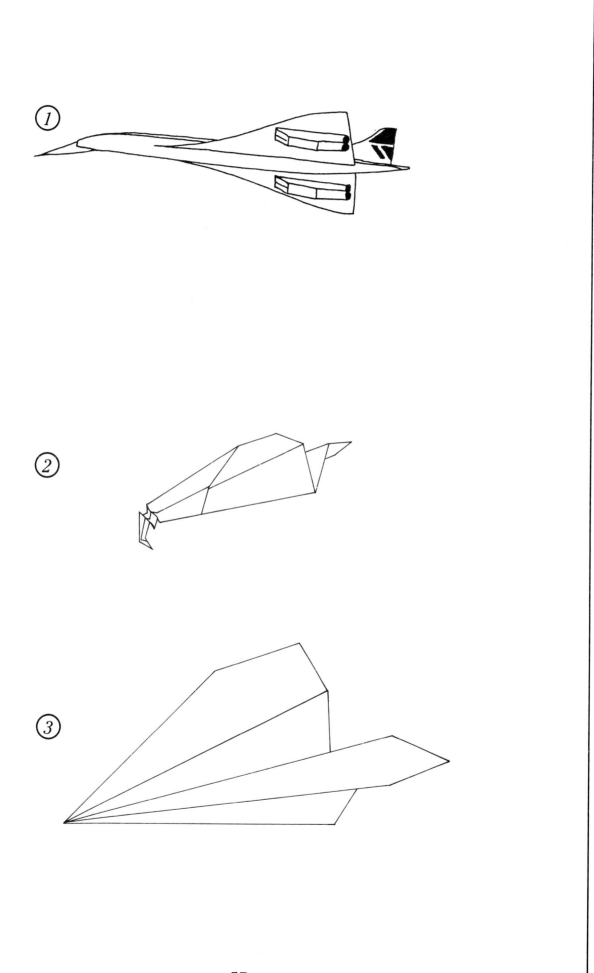

28

HANG-GLIDERS

Let's look at how hang-gliders solve the problems of flexible surfaces.

Modern hang-gliding began when Francis Rogallo (working for NASA on re-entry vehicles) discovered that a diamond-shaped flexible sail could be made into a stable flying machine if it was supported along two leading edges and a keel to form a pair of cone-shaped wings converging at the nose of the glider (Figure 1). The wing sections encountered by the air are parabolas, which happen to be reasonably efficient airfoils (Figure 2). Moreover, these airfoils have a greater angle of attack at the wing root than at the wing-tips, creating washout. Since the airfoil sections at the wing-tips are located further back than those at the keel, the wings are also swept back. The combination of these factors gives stability in both the pitch and yaw axes, and no further stabilizing surfaces are required.

Rogallo's design was original intended to allow *Gemini* space capsules to return to land, but NASA eventually opted for splashdown at sea. However, its potential was quickly recognized by adventurous young pilots who assembled polythene and bamboo gliders and launched themselves off Californian sand dunes, to create the sport of hang-gliding.

The world's simplest paper aeroplane
You can investigate the flight stability of the standard Rogallo shape if you make a model that is small enough to hold its shape without stiffening. Cut a piece of paper to the shape shown full size (Figure 3) and bend it into the double conical shape. Add a small piece of Blu-Tack to the nose, and you have what is probably the world's simplest paper aeroplane. It might also qualify as the smallest paper aeroplane since, with care, you can make perfectly stable gliders that will fit into a matchbox.

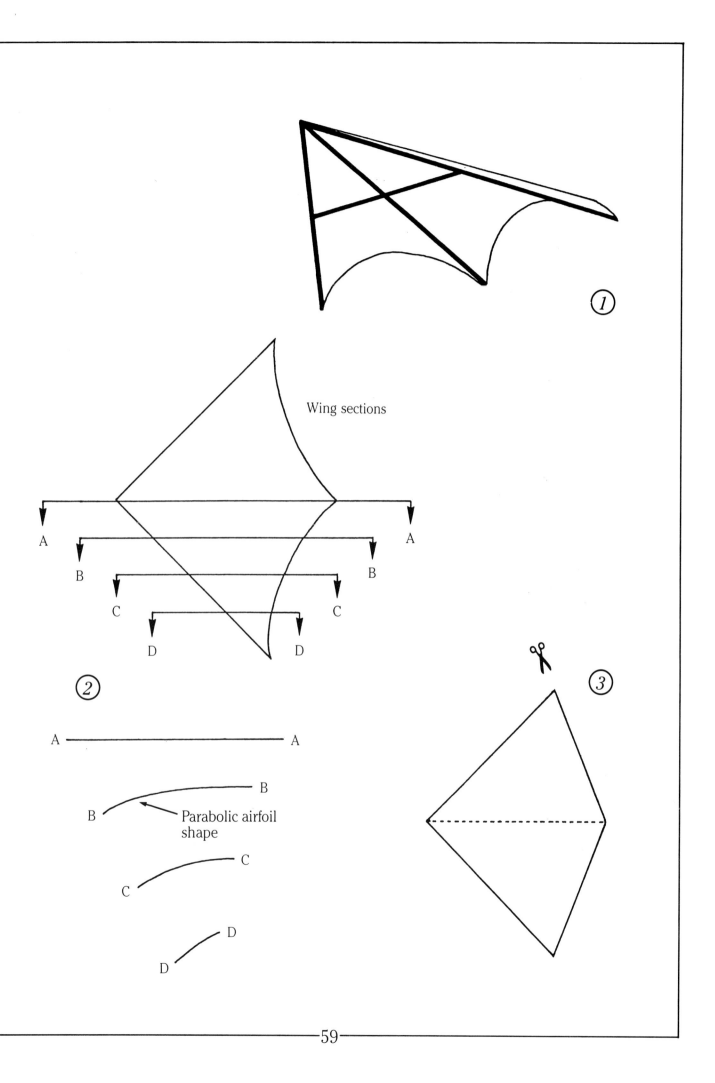

Wing sections

A ————→ A
B ————→ B
C ————→ C
D ————→ D

① ②

A ————————— A

B
B

← Parabolic airfoil
shape

C
C

D
D

③

HANG-GLIDER EVOLUTION

The evolution of hang-glider shapes is relevant to our attempts to improve the performance of the paperang.

Nose angles were increased progressively from about 90° to over 120° as the performance of higher aspect ratio wings was investigated. Sweepback, billow and washout were reduced as designers realized that gliders had more stability than necessary. Today's high-performance hang-gliders look like the one shown in Figure 1. You may have noticed that the paperang is built to a similar shape.

Originally, hang-gliders were controlled in flight purely by the shifting weight of the pilot alone acting on the glider. As aspect ratios and wingspans increased, hang-gliders became more and more cumbersome to turn by weight shifting. Billow shifting was discovered accidentally — some gliders had leading edges that flexed somewhat in flight. When the pilot shifted his weight to one side, the leading edge on that side bent inwards slightly because of the increased load and caused that wing to billow more, creating less lift and more drag. The leading edge on the other side straightened because of the reduced load, flattening the billow with the reverse effect. As soon as it was realized that this was beneficial, gliders were built with mechanisms that exaggerated billow shift. The sail was no longer attached stiffly to the aluminium keel, but to a keel pocket 20 cm or more high, so that the sail could move from side to side (Figure 2). The aluminium cross-spar became detached from the keel, so that in effect the leading edges were free to move from side to side. The result is that modern hang-gliders are controlled aerodynamically by the carefully controlled effects of billow shifting, rather than by the crude method of weight shifting. It is no coincidence that the paperang is also trimmed by billow shifting.

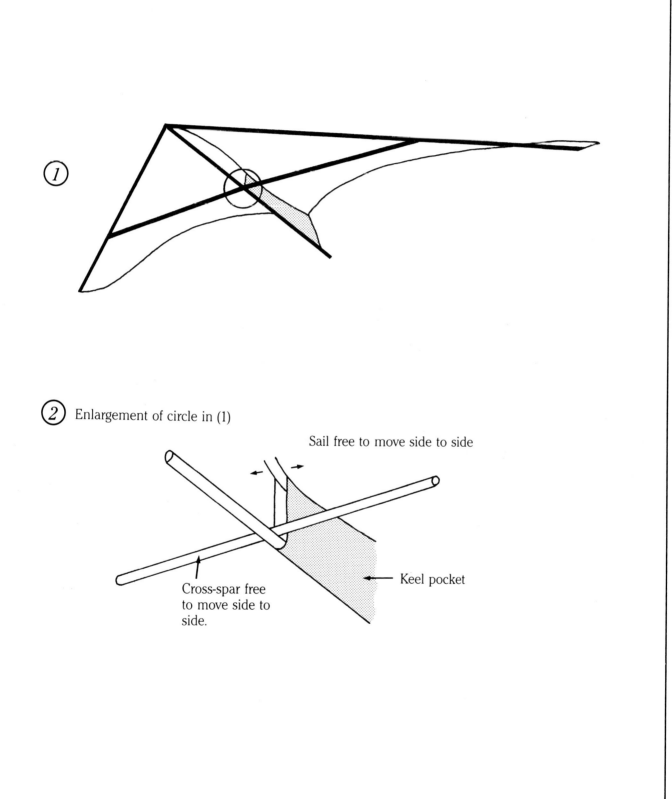

①

② Enlargement of circle in (1)

Sail free to move side to side

Cross-spar free
to move side to
side.

Keel pocket

EPILOGUE

Much as I would have liked to claim that the paperang came to be designed by logical steps, I have to admit it did not really happen that way. As a hang-gliding instructor, I had to give lectures to people who had no knowledge whatsoever of aerodynamics, and teach them enough about flying to allow them to safely control the glider in flight. It seemed to me that paper aeroplanes would provide useful illustrations of hang-glider flight. They could be flown indoors, and trimmed to show the effects of control movements, stalls, and so on. Darts did not look much like hang-gliders, but it took no great leap of the imagination to try to build a paper aeroplane shaped like a hang-glider in order to make the lecture demonstrations more realistic.

Where do we go from here? That depends mainly on what you want to achieve. If, like me, you value the paper aeroplane as something simple that can be made quickly, and consider the most important part of its flight to be the gliding phase when it is not influenced by the strength of the launch, then you will probably find it very difficult to better the paperang concept: a hang-glider-like flying surface braced by tapering leading edge spars.

Paper planes are different from other aircraft only because they are cheap and easy to make — their aerodynamics, with appropriate adjustments for size and flying speed, are exactly the same. The following are some parallels with the world of full-sized aircraft that I have found useful in making better paperangs.

The shape of the wing-tips influences the paperang's performance. The plain, rounded shapes of the standard paperang are quite efficient, especially in light designs, whereas heavier ones can benefit from special shapes such as tip plates. Tip plate design seems to be a promising area of development: they have recently been sprouting from the wings of a range of commercial aircraft from the giant Boeing 747, through the Lear jet and other business aircraft, and down to Burt Rutan's many small kit aircraft designs as well as his recent Voyager aircraft. Tip plates work by reducing wing-tip vortices, and are most effective at high wing loadings. On paperangs they only give slight improvements to the glide ratio, (and I noticed that the loss of the Voyager's tip plates on take-off on its round-the-world flight did not seem to matter much), but because they are vertical surfaces located at the rear of the paperang, they provide extra yaw stability and so allow sweepback to be reduced. They are also useful in trimming, because they can be used as an alternative to billow shifting when correcting for turns, in the same way as the tip plates described for the darts. The disadvantages are that you will always sacrifice some of the wing area at the tips when building the plates, and if the plates are inaccurately made they will badly affect the performance of the paperang.

Another way to improve glide ratio is to reduce drag by flying slowly. This can be achieved by reducing wing loading by maximizing the wing area and minimizing the weight. There are several problems, notably increased flexing (light wings are usually weak, too), but success produces a plane which seems to float rather than just fly. These ideas were brilliantly used in the Gossamer Condor, which won the Kremer Prize for human-powered flight. The forces involved in powered flight are little different from those involved in gliding flight. Basically, the minimum requirement of a powered aircraft is that it should be able to fly horizontally in a straight line at a steady speed. As the glide path of a glider gets closer and closer to the horizontal, its lift:drag ratio becomes larger and larger until when the glide path is horizontal, the L/D equals infinity. At this point, either lift must be infinite, or drag must be equal to zero, neither of which is possible in practice. In powered aircraft a new force, thrust, comes into play which acts in the direction of motion, opposite to drag and cancelling its effects. In level flight, as long as the thrust is equal to the drag, the powered aircraft can be considered equivalent to a glider with no drag. The main design requirement for a man-powered aircraft is therefore that the drag (at the air speed required to produce lift equal to the aircraft's weight) must not exceed the thrust that can be produced by the pilot, so the designer's problem is basically one of drag reduction.

Planes designed previously to win the Kremer Prize attempted to reduce drag by paying great attention to the shape of the aircraft, with every effort being made to prevent wing flexing and to keep bumps and ripples in the aircraft's surface to a minimum. Unfortunately, these designs always turned out to be heavy and required a high air speed for take-off. This in turn increased drag so that most had great difficulty even in achieving take-off. The few that took off flew only short distances before exhausting the pilot or crashing due to control problems. The Gossamer Condor, on the other hand, took advantage of the fact that drag increases with the square of velocity, and minimized it by flying very slowly. This was achieved by concentration on weight reduction, using very light carbon fibre spars arranged in a hang-glider-like structure braced by thin piano wire supporting a flexible membrane similar to cling film. The Gossamer Condor turned out to be so light that take-off was achieved at a walking speed, almost as soon as the pilot started to pedal. The slow flying speed also had the advantage of making low altitude crashes safe, and allowed the minimum necessary strength (and weight) of each of the aircraft's components to be found by experiment, decreasing the weight and flying speed still further. The remaining design problem was to control yaw and roll in the turns necessary to complete the figure of eight course. This was overcome by warping the flexible wings with a system of wires and levers operated by the pilot — not a great leap from billow shifting!

It is interesting to note that in full-sized aircraft, stability (the tendency of an aircraft to return to its original attitude) by definition acts against the attempts of the pilot to change the aircraft's attitude. In other words, stability acts against manoeuvrability. Manoeuvrability, the ability to change direction quickly, is at a premium in military aircraft, and so they have always been built with the minimum of stability. Recent developments in 'fly-by-wire' computer technology have enabled the newest military aircraft to be aerodynamically unstable, their onboard computers acting automatically to correct any deviation from the desired flight path before it goes out of control. Such aircraft can then be turned much more sharply than their stable predecessors. One of the early British unstable experimental aircraft was a Jaguar (a stable ground-attack jet) which had been made unstable by the addition of tons of lead to its tail. Such experiments will strike a chord with the reader who has been experimenting with Blu-Tack as suggested! With paper aeroplanes, however, positive stability on all axes must be provided if the design is to fly in a straight line. The paperang is quite stable in the pitch axis, so that it is easily trimmed out of stalls and dives. On the other hand, it is only just stable in the roll and yaw axes so that it can continue to fly straight if launched with wings level indoors, but will only return slowly to straight flight if the wings are banked. This is what allows the same paperang to fly either straight or in a circle depending on how you launch it, or circle in thermals if you launch it outdoors.

It may be a little over enthusiastic to suggest that paper aeroplane design might be useful in the development of full-sized aircraft, but I believe that the various ideas examined in this book do indicate that careful application of full-sized aerodynamics will result in higher performance paper planes. I hope that this book will inspire you to design your own paper planes, and if you achieve significant improvements over the paperang, I would be delighted to hear from you, care of the publisher. The secret is to make experimental improvements one at a time, test them thoroughly, and record your results as you go along. Happy flying!

GLOSSARY

Aerodynamics The study of the movement of air, especially its behaviour around moving objects.

Air speed The speed at which an object is moving, relative to the surrounding air. (Note that the speed of a flying object relative to the ground is its ground speed.)

Airflow The movement of air past an object.

Airfoil The cross-section of a surface which produces lift at right angles to the direction of motion.

Angle of attack The angle between the direction of motion of a flying surface, and the straight line between its leading and trailing edges.

Aspect ratio A measure of the narrowness of a flying surface, given by the formula Wing-span (m^2)/Wing area (m^2)

Attitude The orientation of an aircraft, defined by its position on the pitch, roll and yaw axes.

Ballast Anything which has the sole purpose of adding weight to the aircraft.

Bank An inclination from the horizontal of a line drawn between the wing-tips.

Billow The upward arch of a flexible wing (eg in hang-gliders and paperangs).

Billow shift A mechanism using relative changes in the billow of the two wings to make aircraft turn.

Centre of gravity The point where the whole of the aircraft's mass can be thought to be concentrated. Sometimes referred to as the balance point.

Dart Simple, low-performance paper aeroplane with pointed nose and approximately triangular wings.

Dihedral The upsweep of wings into a V-shape.

Drag The force arising from the motion of an aircraft through the air which acts directly against the motion of the aircraft.

Force That which will cause an acceleration if applied to an object. Forces have both magnitude and direction.

Form drag Drag that arises from friction between the air and an object moving through it.

Fuselage The body of an aircraft, on which the wings and stablizing surfaces are mounted.

Glide angle The angle between the direction of motion of the glider and the horizontal, often used interchangeably with glide ratio or lift:drag, to describe a glider's performance.

Glide ratio The horizontal distance travelled by a glider divided by the height lost.

Glider An unpowered aircraft.

Hang-glider A flexible-winged glider that is controlled by the weight shift of the pilot suspended from it.

Induced drag Drag that is a by-product of lift generation.

Keel The deep valley (V-shaped in cross-section) between the wings in typical paper darts. The central longitudinal aluminium tube in a hang glider.

Lamination The process by which strong materials can be built up by glueing together layers of thin material, as in plywood.

Leading edge The forward edge of a flying surface.

Lift The force acting at right angles to the direction of motion produced by surfaces moving through the air.

Loop A flying manoeuvre in which the aircraft describes a vertical circular path.

Parabolic conical section The intersection of a plane surface and a cone in certain directions will be along a curved line known as a parabola. This curve in the context of hang-gliders and paperangs approximates an airfoil shape.

Pitch The 'nose-up'-'nose-down' axis of an aircraft.

Pressure Defined as force (in newtons)/area (in m^2). On a given wing, lift is the pressure difference between the air above and below the wing divided by the wing area.

Prototype The first of a new design.

Resultant The force that is equal to the combined effect of two or more forces. It is calculated by vector addition of the component forces.

Roll The rotation of an aircraft around its longitudinal axis (which is therefore called the roll axis).

Sink rate The vertical downwards speed of the glider (in metres per second).

Spar The structural beam that supports a flying surface.

Stability The term which describes the tendency of an aircraft to return to its original flight path if it is disturbed. Positively stable (or simply 'stable') aircraft do this, negatively stable (or 'unstable') aircraft deviate even more from the original flight path, whereas neutrally stable aircraft continue along the new direction.

Stall The condition that arises when the angle of attack becomes so great that the air cannot move smoothly over the top surface of the wing, resulting in a sudden loss of lift and increase in drag. An aircraft which stalls loses height rapidly and usually rotates into a nose-down attitude.

Stall angle The angle of attack at which a flying surface stalls, typically around 20°.

Streamlining The shaping of objects so that they can move through the air with minimum drag.

Sweepback Where the wing-tips are further back than the wing root.

Thermal A bubble or column of air which rises because it is warmer (and therefore less dense) than the surrounding air.

Tip plate A vertical surface at the wing-tip. Properly designed, it can improve the performance of an aircraft.

Trailing edge The rearward edge of a flying surface.

Trim The minor adjustment of flying surfaces to achieve a desired flying performance.

Turbulence The random movements of air disturbed by gusts or moving objects.

Vector A mathematical concept referring to anything that has both magnitude and direction. Force and speed are vectors.

Washout The property of a wing whereby the angle of attack of the wing-tips is less than that of the wing root.

Wing area Defined as the area in m^2 of the plan view (ie the view from above) of the wing.

Wing loading Defined as the weight of the glider divided by the wing area. All other factors being equal, the higher the wing loading, the higher the flying speed of the glider.

Wing-root Where it joins the fuselage, or the centre line between the two wings where there is no fuselage.

Wing-tip The part of the wing furthest from the fuselage or centre line.

Yaw The rotation of an aircraft around the vertical or yaw axis.